CITYSPOTS

FEZ

Thomas Cook

WHAT'S IN YOUR GUIDEBOOK?

Independent authors Impartial up-to-date information from our travel experts who meticulously source local knowledge.

Experience Thomas Cook's 165 years in the travel industry and guidebook publishing enriches every word with expertise you can trust.

Travel know-how Thomas Cook has thousands of staff working around the globe, all living and breathing travel.

Editors Travel-publishing professionals, pulling everything together to craft a perfect blend of words, pictures, maps and design.

You, the traveller We deliver a practical, no-nonsense approach to information, geared to how you really use it.

ABOUT THE AUTHOR

Victoria Gill spent her teenage years living and travelling in the Middle East and North Africa. A globetrotter who has written about travel for *Hedonist's Guides* and *Harper's Bazaar* as well as a range of coffee table books, she has also contributed to *Time Out* and *Luxos* publications. Victoria works as a broadcaster and consultant for TV production companies including Princess Productions and talkbackTHAMES.

CITYSPOTS

FEZ

Victoria Gill

Written by Victoria Gill

Published by Thomas Cook Publishing
A division of Thomas Cook Tour Operations Limited
Company registration No: 1450464 England
The Thomas Cook Business Park, 9 Coningsby Road
Peterborough PE3 8SB, United Kingdom
Email: books@thomascook.com, Tel: +44 (0)1733 416477
www.thomascookpublishing.com

Produced by The Content Works Ltd
Aston Court, Kingsmead Business Park, Frederick Place
High Wycombe, Bucks HP11 1LA
www.thecontentworks.com

Series design based on an original concept by Studio 183 Limited

ISBN: 978-1-84848-038-4

Series Editor: Lucy Armstrong
Production/DTP: Steven Collins

Printed and bound in Spain by GraphyCems

Cover photography (Bab Bou Jeloud) © Mark Karrass/Corbis

CONTENTS

SYMBOLS KEY

The following symbols are used throughout this book:

ⓐ address ⓣ telephone ⓕ fax
ⓦ website address ◷ opening times

The following symbols are used on the maps:

i	information office	■	points of interest
✈	airport	O	city
+	hospital	O	large town
	police station	○	small town
	bus station	=	motorway
	railway station	—	main road
✝	cathedral	—	minor road
❶	numbers denote featured cafés & restaurants	—	railway

Hotels and restaurants are graded by approximate price as follows:
£ budget price **££** mid-range price **£££** expensive

Abbreviations used in addresses:

av. avenue
blvd boulevard
pl. place (square)

▶ *Bou Inania Medersa is in Morocco's largest* medina

INTRODUCING Fez

Introduction

Nothing quite prepares you for Fez. The city is a window to the past and a bewitching portal to another world. With a history spreading over three millennia, Morocco's former capital is the modern-day spiritual and cultural epicentre of its country, and one of the most unique places to visit on earth.

An ancient walled city combining jaw-dropping architecture with excellent shopping, Fez is a captivating blend of old and new. Its Medina is both the biggest *medina* and the largest car-free urban zone in the world, with around 9,000 interweaving lanes and passageways exuding atmosphere, creativity and beauty. There is a brooding, simmering intensity to the place, with its narrow alleys and gleaming minarets; every glimpse is a privilege, and every moment is an explosion of colour, scent, taste and sound. Above this sprawling labyrinth stand fortifications and burial sites that are yet another reminder of Fez's fascinating past.

In 2008, Fez celebrated its 1,200th year, and today it is a city on the cusp of change. Rising up among the tombs and the traditions, the religion and the ramparts, there is a newfound sense of optimism. Another face of Fez is the gleaming Ville Nouvelle – a fine example of a cityscape that could belong anywhere in southern Europe and an area that's buzzing with life at night. Wave after wave of entrepreneurs are opening stylish *riads*, cafés and boutiques in the ancient Medina. Today, Fez is less associated with the hat it once produced than for its standing among the globe's cultural elite.

Fez's mystery has long been compared with a bride on her marriage night seductively lifting her veils. These days, the city feels like a secret that's been simmering for so long it's set to explode.

Dawn view of the city of Fez

When to go

An atmospheric destination whatever the weather, Fez is in its prime during spring (March and April) and autumn (September and October), when the temperature is consistently pleasant and all of its attractions can be enjoyed to the full. Be careful of visiting during Ramadan (see page 12) as Muslims fast in daylight hours and opening times in the Medina and other attractions are subject to change.

SEASONS & CLIMATE

Fez's climate varies significantly between the seasons. In July and August, temperatures can soar to a humid 38°C (100°F). In winter, between December and February, they can plummet to a challenging 4°C (39°F); *riads* (traditional Moroccan dwellings with interior courtyard gardens) whistle with cold and locals don their thickest *jellabas* (floor-length, one-piece garments). That said, if you wish to avoid the tourist crowds, these are the times when you're least likely to run into them. Spring and autumn are the high seasons, with temperatures averaging a pleasant 27°C (80°F).

ANNUAL EVENTS

February

Le Festival de Fès de Musique Andalouse Marocaine (Andalusian Music Festival of Fez) On the last weekend in February, this celebration of Andalusian music takes place in the city's hotels and squares and features the finest classical musicians. ⓐ La Commune Urbaine de Fès, blvd Alalaouiyine ⓣ (035) 65 12 58

April

Festival d'Art Culinaire (Festival of Culinary Arts) This three-day exploration of all things culinary sees local and international experts covering everything from Mauritian cooking to the history of the Tea Ceremony to molecular gastronomy. There are cookery classes, picnics and tastings. ⓐ Oued Souaffine ⓣ (035) 74 05 35 ⓦ www.festivalartculinaire.com

Festival de Fès de la Culture Soufie (Fez Festival of Sufi Culture) Fez has always had strong Sufi traditions, and this week-long festival explores the cultural face of mystical Islam, with concerts, seminars, exhibitions and screenings across town. ⓐ Immeuble 6, Appartement 3, av. Moulay el-Kamel ⓣ (035) 65 39 52 ⓦ www.par-chemins.org

Grand Prix de SAR La Princesse Lalla Meryem The Women's Tennis Association's week-long stop in Fez sees some of the world's greatest tennis players battling it out at the Henri Leconte Tennis Academy (see page 34). ⓣ (035) 65 58 36 ⓕ (035) 72 60 62 ⓦ www.frmt.ma

May

Festival de la Fez de la Musique Malhoune (Malhoune Music Festival of Fez) This three-day music festival spans the first weekend of May, with free concerts across many of the Medina's prettiest open spaces. ⓐ Association Fez Saïss, Sidi el-Khayat, Batha ⓣ (035) 63 54 00

June

World Sacred Music Festival The best world music performers around the globe enrich the city (see page 14).

July

Festival of Amazigh/Berber Culture A colourful event that celebrates all things Berber. It culminates in one of the finest *fantasias* – or horse shows – in Morocco. ⓐ Association Fez Saïss, Sidi el-Khayat, Batha ⓣ (035) 63 54 00

August

Ramadan This thirty-day religious festival is the most important in the Arab world. Muslims fast every day during daylight, and there may be changes to opening times in the Medina and Fez el-Jdid.

September

Festival of Fantasia An early September festival that gives Berber horsemen a chance to show off their skills.

A Berber horseman rides in the Festival of Fantasia

Moulay Idriss Moussem This annual pilgrimage to the most holy site in Morocco attracts thousands.

November

Fez Jazz in Riads Festival Local rappers, Puerto Rican salsa stars and American blues divas perform in venues across the city.
ⓐ Fondation Esprit de Fès, Sidi el-Khayat ⓣ (035) 74 05 35
ⓦ www.fesjazz.com

PUBLIC HOLIDAYS

Year-by-year dates for Muslim holidays (*) can vary by as much as a month, as they are based on the lunar calendar.

New Year's Day 1 Jan

Fatih Mouharram (Islamic New Year) 18 Dec 2009; 7 Dec 2010; 26 Nov 2011*

Aïd al-Mawlid (The Prophet's Birthday) 9 Mar 2009; 26 Feb 2010; 15 Feb 2011*

Labour Day 1 May

Throne Day 30 July

Oued Eddahab Allegiance Day 14 Aug

Revolution Day 20 Aug

The King's Birthday 21 Aug

Ramadan 21 Aug–19 Sept 2009; 11 Aug–8 Sept 2010; 1 Aug–29 Aug 2011*

Eid El Fitr (two days) 27 & 28 Nov 2009; 9 & 10 Sept 2010; 30 & 31 Aug 2011*

Green March Day 6 Nov

World Sacred Music Festival

Every June, Fez comes alive with the sound of classical guitars, string quartets and African drums as the globe's leading world music stars gather for concerts, exhibitions, performances and talks during the World Sacred Music Festival.

Big names such as Ravi Shankar and Youssou N'Dour rub shoulders with Sufi brotherhoods and political activists during this week-long programme, which is run by an artistic director selected from the global arts arena. With events ranging from intimate performances under a Barbary oak in the gardens of the Batha Museum (see page 68) to large-scale productions viewed by thousands in the environs of the Bab al-Makina Palace, the festival is considered the premier world sacred music event.

Indeed, such is its renown that America, France and the UK have been inspired to emulate its success, and the festival has been recognised by the United Nations for its role in promoting cross-cultural dialogue.

From its headquarters in the manicured gardens of **Dar Tazi Palace** (ⓐ Sidi el-Khayat ⓣ (035) 74 05 35) in the Batha area, 'Fez Encounters' is a feature of the Festival that consists of seminars on everything from literature to Sufism. Politicians, luminaries, activists and academics come together to discuss issues central to the world today, from climate change to conflict resolution and urban cityscapes. Elsewhere, the popular 'Sufi Nights' sees brotherhoods and whirling Dervishes from the mystical tradition of Sufism come together for chanting and music.

The World Sacred Music Festival not only encapsulates the soul of Fez but the true spirit of cultures from across the globe.

For anyone who feels inspired to join in, there are numerous instrument-makers in town to furnish you with the tools of song. ⓐ Fondation Esprit de Fès, Sidi Al Khayat ⓣ (035) 74 05 35 ⓦ www.fesfestival.com

▲ *Tariqa Harraqia of Taza perform at Fez's World Sacred Music Festival*

History

Fez's story is as intricate as its labyrinth of winding streets. The right bank of the Oued river was settled in AD 789 by Moulay Idriss, and it was his son Moulay Idriss II who officially founded Fez in 809. Soon afterwards, refugees from the Andalusian region of Spain gave the name to its oldest district, Al-Andalous, and they were joined by Muslims from Tunisia. The city soon became an important trading post.

With the accession of the mighty Merenid dynasty, which reinstated Fez as the capital of Morocco, the 'new quarter' of Fez el-Jdid was established in 1276 as a fortification and a home for the city's burgeoning Jewish community. Thanks to a relatively stable couple of hundred years, the 17th century saw the Saadi family able to position Fez as the most important trading route in Morocco, a vital hub for merchandise travelling through Africa to Europe.

As national identity crystallised, the urge for independence from any invading force increased. The opposition to Morocco's treaty with France in 1912 was particularly strong, especially when the French moved the capital from Fez to Rabat. However, the occupation ushered in an era of modernity as the Ville Nouvelle was built. With its open layout and modern architecture, it pointed to a progressive future.

As the more moneyed citizens moved to this new area, the less prosperous classes either remained in or moved back to the Medina. By the 1980s, the place had become run down and neglected; its designation as a UNESCO World Heritage site in 1981 seemed to signify hope for the future rather than recognition of any current achievement. When Mohammed VI ascended the throne in 1999, he began an aggressive campaign to save Morocco's treasures and legacy, which kick-started a restoration programme. Today, much of Fez's fascination comes from its being both rooted in the past and on the point of massive change.

Colourful mosaics and brass doors are just some of the treasures of Fez

Lifestyle

In Fez, the influences of religion pervade everyday life. Many Moroccan Muslims pray five times daily and make frequent visits to the mosque. Blasphemy is taboo in normal discourse, and alcohol is forbidden in Islam, and thus generally frowned upon.

The standard socialising model consists of Moroccan men sitting outside cafés, chatting and people-watching over cigarettes, coffee and mint tea. Fassis (residents of Fez) believe that the finest food is prepared in the home, so you won't see many Moroccans enjoying lavish, drawn-out suppers in the city's restaurants. What you will see is lunch on the go in a café or at a street stand.

Promenading is also a local pastime, and you'll see families of all generations wandering along Avenue Hassan II in the Ville Nouvelle or the streets of the Medina at night.

Fez has two contrasting faces and two markedly different lifestyles: the traditional Medina and Fez el-Jdid, and the more modern Ville Nouvelle. While, in the Medina, most women wear head coverings and *jellabas*, you will see women in more cosmopolitan dress in the Ville Nouvelle. In the most modern parts of the city you might find scantily clad teenagers jumping in your taxi en route to a house party – these same girls might have been wearing head-to-toe garb just one hour before in the old town.

Within the Medina and around Fez el-Jdid, the majority of Moroccans work as artisans, shopkeepers, tour guides or in hospitality. Business is often a family matter, with different generations all lending a hand. Ville Nouvelle's citizens are more likely to work in white-collar professions, with computing and technology a particularly burgeoning trade. You'll see far more women going to work here than in the Medina.

To counteract the negative effects of the strong work ethic, Moroccans head for the *hammams*, as they have done for centuries, or out to the open areas around Ifrane (see page 123) to savour the fresh air.

Many Fassis are artisans specialising in one craft or trade

Culture

Fez's culture isn't confined to picture frames and museum walls – it's all around you. Some of the most highly skilled artisans in the world work in the streets, keeping alive centuries-old skills and traditions. The massive vats of the tanneries, the instrument-makers, the city's last remaining blacksmith and the almost unique sight of brocade being stitched by hand form an impressive patchwork of street theatre.

Fez is known as a centre of creativity and intellectualism, much of which derives from Morocco's colourful history. It would take an acute Western ear to be able to differentiate between the Arabic and Berber dialects that are spoken here, but you'll recognise French, which is a remnant of the days when the country was a protectorate of France.

Today the city's cultural output goes from strength to strength. In addition to the many annual festivals (see page 10), cultural organisations such as the Institut Français de Fès (see page 94) offer performances, talks and film screenings. Smaller associations such as Café Clock (see page 78) present literary talks and music evenings, while accomplished local musicians play at the city's most expensive restaurants.

Institutions such as the Batha and Nejjarine Museums (see page 68) vividly illustrate centuries of Fassi and Berber lifestyles and achievements. To get a truly meaningful insight into the city's depth and variety of culture, check out the many classes and walks on offer.

Inner courtyard of the Musée Nejjarine des Arts

EVERYDAY ARCHITECTURE

The architecture that was designed around Fez's daily life is one of the city's main attractions. Elaborate and profoundly beautiful, it also serves as a practical guide to how Fassis lived in the past.

A curiosity that should not be missed is the *funduq*, or *caravanserie*. Part inn, part stable, their lower area housed horses while their masters slept in the bedrooms above.

Much of Morocco's character is revealed by focussing on what lies beneath the surface. This is true of its buildings also: the standard design of the *riad* draws attention sharply to its central point. Standard interior décor sees innocuous exteriors hide exquisite mosaics, breathtaking calligraphic ornamentation, carved cedar, fountains and stained glass. Windows are forsaken in favour of small peepholes with bars, enabling women to see out without being seen. Looking posts above entrances are also common. Craftswomen would do business for decades without ever having to come face to face with their associates.

Most of the grandest houses have three doors – one for horses, another for people, and, to the side, a small door through which an eldest son would be able to sneak his lover without the overt approval of his parents. Front doors often display superstitious decorations such as evil eyes and hand symbols to ward off bad spirits and intention.

Traditional knife sharpening in the souks

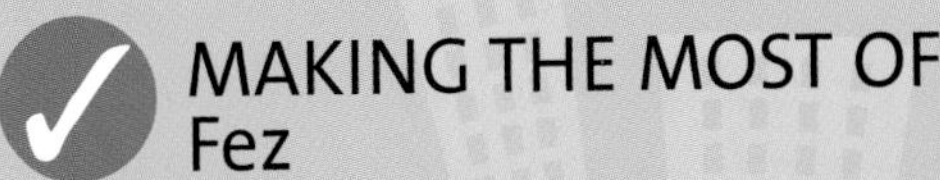

MAKING THE MOST OF Fez

Shopping

Fez's Medina must rank among the world's most interesting places to shop: if you don't have difficulties closing your suitcase when you leave, then you're unusual. You can spend days exploring the countless shops, bartering, chatting, sipping mint tea and occasionally being barged by mules or donkeys. Common buys are ornaments, furniture, embroidery and the argan oil that's been keeping Berber women's wrinkles at bay for centuries. Prices are low compared to Europe and Marrakech. There's something for every budget, from homemade honey to antique dressers dating back 700 years. If it can be crafted from metal, clay, leather, embroidery or wood then you can probably find it here.

The Medina's two main arteries are Talaa Kebira and Talaa Segira, meaning 'big pleasure' and 'small pleasure'. These are great for browsing, with an array of shops spanning the stylish to the traditional to the downright bizarre. As you get deeper into the Medina, however, streets narrow, paths become more labyrinthine and areas, or *souks*, start to become more specialised. Apart from the Talaa Kebira and the Talaa Segira, most areas of the Medina are divided by the types of wares they sell. Some, such as the dyers' street or toolmakers' *souk*, make for amazing spectacles. In the leather region you can pick up a beautifully crafted wallet, handbag or briefcase at a steal, and in the Henna Souk (see page 64) you'll find some of the best pottery in Morocco. For consumables, head for the Attarine (spice) market (see page 73), or the Kaat Smen (condiments) market (see page 72).

Elsewhere, *babouches* (Moroccan shoes) have their own area, as do bridal belts and elaborate gowns. Morocco is also known

Bags and carpets on offer in the souks

Babouches *are a popular and useful souvenir*

USEFUL SHOPPING PHRASES

What time do the shops open/close?
A quelle heure ouvrent/ferment les magasins?
Ah kehlur oovr/fehrm leh mahgazhang?

How much is this?
C'est combien?
Cey combyahng?

Can I try this on?
Puis-je essayer ceci?
Pweezh ehssayeh cerssee?

My size is ...
Ma taille (clothes)/ma pointure (shoes) est ...
Mah tie/mah pooahngtewr ay ...

I'll take this one, thank you
Je prends celui-ci/celle-ci, merci
Zher prahng serlweesi/sehlsee, mehrsee

for good value jewellery; the Medina has a small *kissariat* (covered *souk*) but the one found next to the Mellah in Fez el-Jdid has more variety (see page 91). Better still, head to Meknes (see page 106), where the gold and silver selection is wider and even more attractively priced.

For household products, more practical essentials and alcohol, however, head to the Ville Nouvelle (see page 98).

Eating & drinking

At the end of the last millennium, Moroccan food deservedly assumed its place as a world cuisine of immense quality, creativity and interest. Preparing good food is a labour of love here. All over the country you'll find dishes such as steaming *tagines* that have been prepared and baked for hours in clay pots, delicately spiced and wonderfully fresh. But the *tagine* is only the tip of the culinary iceberg. For example, *ferakh maamer*, which consists of chicken stuffed with seasoned couscous and then casseroled in a honey sauce, also demonstrates exactly why Moroccan food is so highly regarded.

Fez, of course, produces its own variations on national favourites. Its signature dish is the *pastilla* – a sweet-and-savoury pastry delight sprinkled with almonds and cinnamon and delicately filled with layers of either creamy pigeon or chicken. These layers are separated by *warka*, delicate pancakes infused with cinnamon. If you fancy some really exotic recipe combinations, try the fabulously vivid street food in the markets.

If you want to experience a wide range of Fez food options in a short period, head indoors. Many of the finer restaurants offer

PRICE CATEGORIES

The restaurant price guides used in the book indicate the approximate cost of a three-course meal for one person, excluding drinks.

£ up to 120dh **££** 120–300dh **£££** over 300dh

Try a succulent Moroccan lamb or chicken tagine

set banquet-style menus with a selection of dishes. Generally starters are comprised of a variety of cooked and fresh salads.

USEFUL DINING PHRASES

I would like a table for ... people
Je voudrais une table pour ... personnes
Zher voodray ewn tabl poor ... pehrson

Waiter/waitress!
Monsieur/Mademoiselle, s'il vous plaît!
M'sewr/madmwahzel, sylvooplay!

May I have the bill, please?
L'addition, s'il vous plaît!
Laddyssyawng, sylvooplay!

Could I have it well-cooked/medium/rare please?
Je le voudrais bien cuit/à point/saignant, s'il vous plaît?
Zher ler voodray beeang kwee/ah pwang/saynyang, sylvooplay?

I am a vegetarian. Does this contain meat?
Je suis végétarien (végétarienne). Est-ce que ce plat contient de la viande?
Zher swee vehzhehtarianhg (vehzhehtarien). Essker ser plah kontyang der lah veeahngd?

These are followed by a *pastilla* and then *brochettes* (skewered meat), or *tagines* with couscous. All of this is finished off with a pastry or serving of fruit.

Alcohol is not widely drunk and you'll struggle to find it served unless you visit the top restaurants and hotel bars and clubs. Decent cocktails are only available in the trendiest joints, such as Mezzanine (see page 92) and L'Alcazar (see page 81) of the Riad Fez stable. The good-time beverages here – and ones that never result in street punch-ups and post-holiday recriminations – are fresh fruit juices, strong coffee and mint tea. The latter, also known as 'Whiskey Moroccain', is usually served hot in a glass, with oodles of fresh mint and even more sugar, sometimes accompanied by a pastry or dessert.

If you find that you don't take wholeheartedly to a non-stop diet of Moroccan food, there is a growing number of international establishments opening up. You can try a camel burger followed by lemon tart in Café Clock (see page 78), sushi at Kiotori (see page 100) or French cuisine at Le Majestic (see page 102).

Although Moroccans tend to eat late, at around 21.00, most restaurants start serving around 19.00. Please note that many of the city's cafés and restaurants do not have set opening hours, and some do not possess a telephone. If you wish to visit an establishment for which no opening hours and/or no phone number is given, it's wisest to drop by in advance and make a booking.

Entertainment & nightlife

Fez is not a Marrakech, a Las Vegas or an Ibiza – generally tourists flock here more for cultural attractions and shopping than for its discos and bars (of which there are relatively few). But that does not mean that the city lacks nightlife: there's plenty here to keep you entertained in the evening.

A lavish dinner in one of the many historic *riads* in the Medina should come high on most visitors' itineraries. Romantic and atmospheric, a long banquet-style supper in one of the city's better hotels (see page 36) is an experience not to be missed. In many places you can eat alfresco, allowing you to people-watch as well as appreciate the city's architecture and culture over dinner. Some more upmarket venues offer live classical music performed by leading local musicians, while the gaudier ones such as **Al-Fassia** (ⓐ 21 rue Salaj ⓣ (035) 63 73 14) feature elaborate floorshows with belly-dancers. Some think these spectacles commercial and kitschy; others find them hugely entertaining.

It's also within hotels that you'll find the bars in the Medina. While the city is far from being the ideal place for a pub crawl, you can still enjoy the stylish design of venues such as L'Alcazar (see page 81) or drink your fill of the atmosphere in Fez's only pub in the Hotel Batha (see page 81). Savouring a drink on one of the Medina's many terraces as evening falls can be a memorable experience.

Beyond the Medina, virtually all the nightclubs in the Ville Nouvelle are located underground in hotels. However, things are changing, and Fez acquired its first style bar in 2008 – Mezzanine

Savour the tastes of a Moroccan feast in a riad *in the Medina*

(see page 92) lies just beyond the city walls, serving tapas and cocktails on three slick levels and a buzzing terrace.

For conventional nightlife, head to the Ville Nouvelle. As you mix with the young locals, you'll get a taste of new Morocco and witness how a Western-style night out looks in such an esoteric setting. It would certainly be a shame to not to sample one of the city's discos just once. You can choose between the teeny-bopper arena of Felix (see page 102), the edgier, older, lounge feel of Volubilis (see page 104) or the pricey exclusivity of La Phoebus at Jnane Palace (see page 103). The nightclubs usually get going around 23.00 and close between 03.00 and 04.00.

For nocturnal fun of a more sober – but no less enjoyable – nature, try joining the evening promenade up and down Avenue Hassan II in the Ville Nouvelle. This is a spruced-up boulevard where many locals form a procession of night-time ramblers. Just turning up and walking alongside several generations of the same family is a great way to bulldoze those cultural barriers. It certainly feels better in the morning.

Sport & relaxation

Fez's sporting menu is on the skimpy side, with the exception of the Henri Leconte Tennis Academy and Mas Football Stadium (see below). For relaxation, the city's *hammams* are abundant and wide-ranging in their scope.

SPECTATOR SPORTS

Football

The **Mas Stadium** (ⓐ Complexe Sportif de Fès, route de Sefrou ⓦ www.massawi.com), is home to the almighty, all-conquering Massawi football team, aka The Tigers. It can accommodate up to 45,000 fans.

Tennis

Henri Leconte Tennis Academy Big matches are played here, but, with courts, pools and a gym, this is a draw for spectators and participants alike. ⓐ El-Merja, Commune Urbaine de Zouagha-Moulay Yacoub ⓣ (035) 65 58 36 ⓦ www.hlacademy.net

PARTICIPATION SPORTS

Golf

Royal Golf de Fès (ⓐ Route d'Immouzzer ⓣ (035) 66 52 10 ⓦ www.royalgolfdefes.ma) is located 17 km (10 ½ miles) outside the town centre and is a vast course with great greens and good views.

Horseriding

Royal Equestrian Club of Fez A celebrated riding club just

HEAD FOR A HAMMAM

As well as being a must-try experience in itself, a trip to a *hammam* will leave you feeling invigorated and relaxed. The following is a selection of just some of the best eye-opening, pore-opening venues:

Ain Azliten Hammam Well maintained and comparatively cheap, this is the perfect place to get in a lather. ⓐ Talaa Kebira ⓛ 06.00–23.00

Nausikaa Spa A *haute couture* spa that opened in 2008, this sprawling area encompasses swimming pools, plentiful relaxation areas and a state-of-the-art *hammam* among charming gardens. ⓐ Av. Bahnini ⓣ (035) 61 00 06 ⓦ www.nausikaa-spa.com ⓛ 07.00–21.00

Seffarine Hammam Considered a pearl among the Medina's *hammams*, this place gives an authentic insight into age-old local life. ⓐ Seffarine Square ⓛ 06.00–00.00 men; 08.00–22.00 women

outside Fez. ⓐ Domaine Equestre Aïn Amyer, route d'Imouzzer ⓣ (061) 30 86 84 ⓦ www.marocrandocheval.com

Swimming

There is a municipal pool (open mid-June to mid-Sept) on Avenue des Sports, just west of the train station. The **Hotel Menzeh Zalagh** (ⓐ 10 rue Mohammed Diouri ⓣ (035) 93 22 34) has an outdoor pool, as does Sofitel Palais Jamaï (see page 38), where a dip is included in the price of lunch.

Accommodation

Fez's accommodation spectrum ranges from the intimate to the corporate. There are 5-star big boys offering swimming pools and 24-hour room service and intimate, exquisitely beautiful *riads* whose owners will treat you like a long-lost relative.

Ville Nouvelle's options tend towards fairly unimaginative hotels with good facilities and varying service standards; by contrast, the Medina has just two hotels alongside an array of charming and beautiful *riads*. The latter are probably the better option for most, both for the location and the experience.

Some of the top *riads* offer *hammams*, pools and evening classes, alongside antique features and four-poster beds. Those that don't offer all the trimmings can still be captivatingly beautiful, with exquisite mosaics, arcing ceilings, shuttered windows, marble floors and stunning cedar and brass fittings. Many are family-run and exude a home-from-home feel.

HOTELS & *RIADS*

Hotel Batha £ The only conventional hotel within the Medina, the 3-star Batha is a great value option which also offers space for sunbathing and room service. Rooms are on the small side

PRICE CATEGORIES
Prices for a single night in a double room for two people are:
£ up to 600dh **££** 600–1,300dh **£££** over 1,300dh

Ornate elegance at Dar Seffarine

but the complex is big, with enclaves for eating and drinking. ⓐ Pl. de L'Istiqlal, Medina ⓣ (035) 63 48 24

Hotel Ibis Moussafir Fès £ Pleasant, no-nonsense, reliable 3-star hotel next to the train station in the Ville Nouvelle, with a pool and space for sunbathing. ⓐ Av. des Almohades, pl. de la Gare, Ville Nouvelle ⓣ (035) 65 19 02 ⓦ www.ibishotel.com

Pension Dar Bouanania £ The basics are all present and correct in this charismatic, cost-effective *riad* that's perfect for those who want to lay their hat close to the Medina. Bedrooms sleep up to four while bathrooms are en suite or exclusive to the key-holder. ⓐ 21 Derb ben Salem, Talaa Kebira, Medina ⓣ (035) 63 72 82

Riad Myra £ One of the most popular of Fez's *riads*, Myra incorporates four-poster beds and is brimming with antiques. It's situated around a charming courtyard in traditional surroundings. ⓐ 13 rue Salaj, Batha, Medina ⓣ (035) 74 00 00 ⓦ www.riadmyra.com

Dar Seffarine ££ Good value, clean and pleasant rooms in an exquisite 600-year-old *riad*. High on atmosphere, it is set within the heart of the Medina, on Seffarine Square. ⓐ 14 Derb Sbaa Louyate, Seffarine, Medina ⓣ (071) 11 35 28 ⓦ www.darseffarine.com

La Clé de Fès ££ This chic *riad* has contemporary touches in historic surroundings. A fireplace in winter and a pretty swimming pool in summer keep guests seasonally entertained.

ⓐ 21 Derb el-Guebbas, Douh, Medina ⓣ (035) 63 74 99
ⓦ www.riadlacledefes.com

Riad Dar Dmana ££ Carved screens, luxe fabrics and petal-strewn washbasins in *hammam*-style bathrooms are among the features you'll find in the ten bedrooms and suites of this boutique guesthouse. ⓐ 20 rue Salaj, Douh, Batha, Medina ⓣ (035) 74 09 17 ⓦ www.riaddardmana.net

Riad Dar Tafilalet ££ Set within the heart of the Medina, Tafilalet offers the chance to sample the legendary Berber hospitality, not to mention food. There are cookery classes and trips to its sister hotels in the desert. All rooms except one are suites.
ⓐ 17 Derb Miter Zenjfor, Medina ⓣ (035) 63 51 62
ⓦ www.riadtafilalet.com

Riad Saba ££ Value and warmth at this bijou *riad*. All of the bedrooms have Berber styling and most have a spa bath. ⓐ 3 Derb Skallia, Douh, Batha, Medina ⓣ (035) 63 45 23 ⓦ www.riad-saba.com

Sofitel Palais Jamaï ££ An old-school hotel nestled on the hill above the Medina. It has stunning views, 24-hour room service and a pool in which to soak off the summer heat. There are bars, restaurants and a spa. ⓐ Bab Guissa, Medina ⓣ (035) 63 43 31
ⓦ www.sofitel.com

La Maison Bleue £££ Fez's oldest hotel is also its most romantic. Features include one of the city's finest restaurants. ⓐ 2 pl. de l'Istiqlal, Medina ⓣ (035) 63 60 52 ⓦ www.maisonbleue.com

Riad Fès's charming courtyard by night

Riad Fès £££ This luxury *riad* features amazing décor, superior service, fantastic terraces and a trendy bar and restaurant. ⓐ Derb ben Slimane, Zerbtana, Medina ⓣ (035) 94 76 10 ⓦ www.riadfes.com

Riad Laaroussa £££ One of the city's most loved *riads*, this French-run 17th-century beauty has a large open courtyard, bijou *hammam* and sumptuous rooms. ⓐ 3 Derb Bechara, Medina ⓣ (074) 18 76 39 ⓦ www.riad-laaroussa.com

Riad Maison Bleue £££ With three *riads* converted into one, this decadent address features four-poster beds, a plunge pool, two restaurants, a *hammam* and a terrace boasting fantastic views over the Merenid Tombs and Borj Nord. ⓐ 33 Derb el-Mitter, Ain Azliten, Medina ⓣ (035) 74 18 73/39 ⓦ www.maisonbleue.com

Riad Numero 9 £££ Guests rave about this bijou, intimate *riad* with three rooms that make for a truly personal touch. The team here offer fantastic cooking alongside friendly hospitality that ensures you're left wanting for nothing. ⓐ Derb el Masid, Medina ⓣ (035) 63 40 45 ⓦ www.riad9.com

THE BEST OF FEZ

Whether you're in Fez for a week or an afternoon, the city has a variety of easy access, close-proximity attractions that should simply not be missed.

TOP 10 ATTRACTIONS

- **A Stroll through the Medina** The exotic sights, sounds and smells make the Medina a colourful, unique experience (see page 60)

- **The Chouara Tanneries** Among the most remarkable sights (not to mention smells) of the Medina is that of the giant, coloured vats being worked by the tanners, as they have been for a thousand years (see page 64)

- **Bou Inania Medersa** Of all the city's seats of learning, this is the most complete *medersa* (school) you can experience, where intricate mosaics and stunning cedar carvings abound (see page 60)

- **Moulay Idriss Zawiya** As you approach the mausoleum of Fez's architect and the son of its founder, the sense of religious awe heightens (see page 66)

Wooden door detail from the Bou Inania Medersa

- **A Night in a *Riad*** Let your sleep be cloaked in centuries of history as you lie in peerless surroundings with sumptuous mosaics, carved ceilings and four-poster beds (see page 36)

- **Kairaouine Mosque & University** It's said that all roads in Fez lead to Kairaouine. Circle the alleyways surrounding it to catch glimpses of the cool white interiors that can house up to 20,000 worshippers. Next to it is reputedly the oldest university in the world (see page 66)

- **Mellah** Compare the Venetian-style architecture of the new district with its timewarp synagogue and movingly evocative cemetery (see page 88)

- **Musée Nejjarine des Arts** This stunning former VIP Fundouq was restored by UNESCO and is one of the most striking examples of architecture in the city, with a gallery and terrace overlooking the Medina (see page 68)

- **Shopping in the *Souks*** Shopping in Fez is an adventure in itself, where bartering, buying and sightseeing add up to a truly unique experience (see page 24)

- **Relax in a *Hammam*** Get hot and soapy then steamed, exfoliated and massaged in this enduring and therapeutic Moroccan ritual (see page 35)

Suggested itineraries

HALF-DAY: FEZ IN A HURRY

Easy: the Medina. Just a simple stroll will throw up sights and experiences you never imagined possible. Start outside the magnificent Bou Jeloud gates (see page 60) and follow the Talaa Kebira main artery down to Nejjarine Square (see page 66). Next to this is Seffarine (see page 67), where artisans bash out a melodic sound on their assorted pieces of metal. Take tea and cake while people-watching at Cremerie La Place (see page 77) or admiring the view at the Nejjarine Museum Café (see page 77).

1 DAY: TIME TO SEE A LITTLE MORE

Explore the Medina to its fullest. Take in historic monuments such as the Bou Inania Medersa (see page 60), Kairaouine Mosque (see page 66) and the many *caravanseries* or *souks*. Afterwards, spend a little time shopping in the market, and in the evening enjoy a drink at Les Mérinides (see page 92), followed by a Fassi banquet at La Maison Bleue (see page 80).

2–3 DAYS: TIME TO SEE MUCH MORE

On your second morning, explore Fez el-Jdid. Start outside the magnificent palace gates and make your way along the Mellah (see page 88), being sure to check out the synagogue along the way. Explore the ramparts, heading to the Al-Andalous Mosque (see page 82), admiring the huge pottery workshops and taking in the sites of the Medina from the Merenid Tombs (see page 88). In the evening, sample one of Ville Nouvelle's restaurants (see page 100), then dance among the Fassi elite at La Phoebus (see page 103).

Intricate mosaic fountain near Nejjarine Square

LONGER: ENJOYING FEZ TO THE FULL

You now have the opportunity to immerse yourself in Fez's quintessential experience, the Medina. Round off the phenomenon by getting into a lather at a *hammam*. You'll also have time to interweave your days with journeys out of town. Meknes (see page 106), with its neighbouring sites of Volubilis and Moulay Idriss, makes for a brilliant day out or overnight stay. But if you really want to unwind, head for the heights: the Middle Atlas range (see page 118) is only 70 km (43 ½ miles) away.

Something for nothing

Fez's delights are many and varied; just being in the city and observing how it works offers constant free entertainment. The city's architecture and life is all around you, from the minarets to the defunct Water Clock (see page 68) and from the man sleeping under his donkey on Talaa Kebira to housewives filling their buckets with water from the fountain.

The irony of the Medina is that, although it's a giant commercial hub, its most priceless asset is the experience in itself. Just wander the streets, taking in the sights, sounds and smells – whether that's of the Souk Attarine (see page 73), where spices are sold, or the Chouara Tanneries (see page 64). The latter are best taken in from the terraces of the leather shops above. Glimpse bakers with their open fires and breads waiting to be glazed. Poke your head around the door of a primary school class chanting mantras laid out on the blackboard. Marvel at the city's architecture from the many *babs* (city gates) and circle the Kairaouine Mosque (see page 66) during the call to prayer, when glimpses of its calming white interiors can be snatched.

Take a break in the Jnane Sbil (see page 87) on the way to the Mellah (see page 88), or simply sit on the steps of Seffarine Square (see page 67) and listen to the avant-garde brass orchestra of men hammering metal. Take in the looming gates of the palace (see page 82) and wander around the 14th-century Merenid Tombs (see page 88). These are set on the banks of the city and afford wonderful views over the Medina. Observe the toolmakers' district and the carpenters' workshops next to Nejjarine Square (see page 66). Then wander down to the old slave market where

you can ponder the fact that, although many of Fez's wonders are still free, human life is thankfully now accorded its proper value.

Immerse yourself in the hustle and bustle of Seffarine Square

When it pours and when it soars

If you visit Fez in the summer, you'll certainly experience hot temperatures and you might well encounter a downpour. If you visit in winter, you could easily wish you'd packed your thermals. Thankfully, much of the Medina is covered – particularly in the *souks* towards the centre – so rain won't necessarily stop play. Moreover, the architecture itself gives good protection against the elements; the marble interiors of the *riads* keep it cool indoors, while the narrow thoroughfares protect against both rain and sun.

However, if you find yourself in winter with the temperature biting and without a woolly *jellaba* to keep you warm, head to a *hammam* for a few hours for a soak and unwind. Take shelter in one of the city's excellent museums, or simply sip a mint tea and people-watch from the comfort of a café. This is also the prime time to indulge in a sumptuous feast in one of the city's restaurants, such as Dar Saada (see page 78) or La Maison Bleue (see page 80).

In summer the narrow walls of the Fez el-Bali can feel incredibly close, and after a few days you may find yourself craving open spaces. Head to the Jnane Sbil (see page 87) as the locals do, or take a hike around the ramparts. If you're really feeling the heat, visit the more open thoroughfares of Fez el-Jdid (see page 82) or, better still, the Ville Nouvelle (see page 94). Alternatively, revel in the falling temperatures that accompany the setting sun with a drink on one of the Medina's many terraces.

If it's really hot, take a trip to Azrou, Ifrane or Tazzeka (see pages 120, 123 and 126). These are located in the Middle Atlas Mountains, where the air clears and the temperatures drop.

A hammam *in Chefchaouen* *(see page 122)* *in the Rif Mountains*

On arrival

TIME DIFFERENCE

Fez is on Greenwich Mean Time (GMT) all year round.

ARRIVING

By air

Fez's airport, **Fez Saïss** (ⓐ BP A11 ⓣ (035) 62 48 00 ⓦ www.onda.ma) is located around 13 km (8 miles) south of Fez. It has one terminal and a couple of bureaux de change and places to snack. A bus stopping at various points in the Ville Nouvelle costs approximately 5dh and runs four times daily. Taxis operate pretty much around the clock and the journey costs about 30dh.

By rail

Fez's **Gare Ferroviaire** (ⓐ Pl. du Roi Faycal ⓣ (035) 62 50 01

w www.oncf.ma) is situated close to the centre of the Ville Nouvelle and there is always a plentiful supply of taxis waiting outside. The cost of a trip to the Medina is around 8dh. If you are leaving Fez and travelling south you will have to cross the tracks to access the platform. This is perfectly safe.

By road

There are two main bus stations in Fez: **Gare CTM** (t (035) 73 29 92), in the Atlas neighbourhood of the Ville Nouvelle, and **Gare Routière** (t (035) 63 60 32). The latter is just outside the Ain Azliten area of the Medina on Avenue Chefchaouen, and is a large hub with outlets to buy refreshments for your journey. Some people prefer the slightly smarter CTM buses to the independent buses that leave outside the Gare Routière. Each station has taxi ranks right outside.

Fez is a sprawling city with plenty to discover

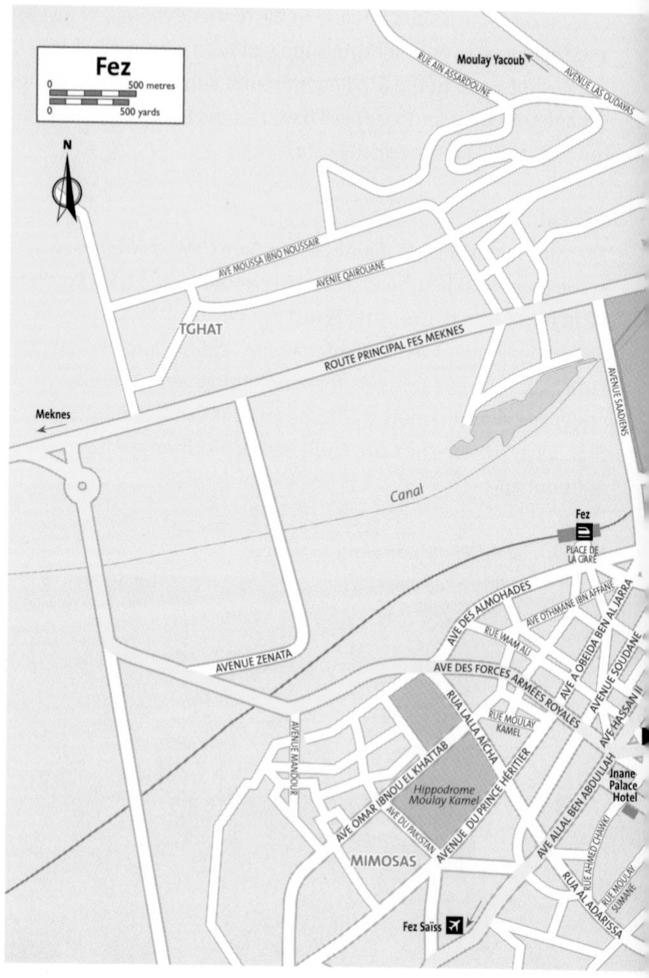
Fez
0
500 metres
0
500 yards
N
Moulay Yacoub
RUE AIN ASSARDOUNE
AVENUE LAS OUDAYAS
AVE MOUSSA IBNO NOUSSAIR
AVENIE QAIROUANE
TGHAT
ROUTE PRINCIPAL FES MEKNES
AVENUE SAADIENS
Meknes
Canal
Fez
PLACE DE LA GARE
AVE DES ALMOHADES
AVE OTHMANE IBN AFFANE
RUE IMAM ALI
AVE A OBEIDA BEN AL JARRA
AVENUE SOUDANE
AVENUE ZENATA
AVE DES FORCES ARMÉES ROYALES
AVE HASSAN II
RUA LALLA AÏCHA
RUE MOULAY KAMEL
AVENUE MANDOUR
AVE OMAR IBNOU EL KHATTAB
Hippodrome Moulay Kamel
AVE DU PAKISTAN
AVENUE DU PRINCE HÉRITIER
AVE ALLAL BEN ABDULLAH
Jnane Palace Hotel
RUE AHMED CHAWKI
RUE MOULAY SLIMANE
RUA AL ADARISSA
MIMOSAS
Fez Saïss

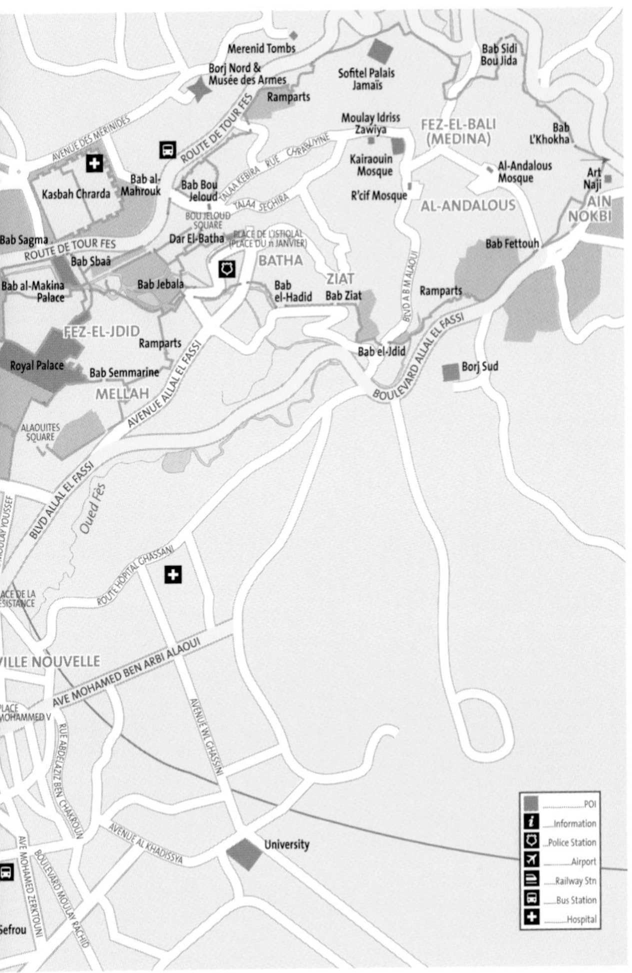
Merenid Tombs
Borj Nord & Musée des Armes
Sofitel Palais Jamaïs
Bab Sidi Bou Jida
Ramparts
Moulay Idriss Zawiya
FEZ-EL-BALI (MEDINA)
Bab L'Khokha
AVENUE DES MERINIDES
ROUTE DE TOUR FES
RUE CHRABLIYINE
Kairaouin Mosque
Al-Andalous Mosque
Art Naji
Kasbah Chrarda
Bab al-Mahrouk
Bab Bou Jeloud
TALAA KEBIRA
TALAA SEGHIRA
R'cif Mosque
AL-ANDALOUS
AIN NOKBI
BOU JELOUD SQUARE
Bab Sagma
ROUTE DE TOUR FES
Dar El-Batha
PLACE DE L'ISTIQLAL (PLACE DU 11 JANVIER)
Bab Fettouh
Bab Sbaâ
BATHA
BLVD A B M ALAOUI
Bab al-Makina Palace
Bab Jebala
Bab el-Hadid
ZIAT
Bab Ziat
Ramparts
FEZ-EL-JDID
Ramparts
AVENUE ALLAL EL FASSI
Bab el-Jdid
BOULEVARD ALLAL EL FASSI
Borj Sud
Royal Palace
Bab Semmarine
MELLAH
ALAOUITES SQUARE
BLVD ALLAL EL FASSI
Oued Fès
ROUTE HOPITAL GHASSANI
VILLE NOUVELLE
AVE MOHAMED BEN ARBI ALAOUI
AVENUE W.L CHASSINI
RUE ABDELAZIZ BEN CHAKROUN
AVENUE AL KHADISSYA
University
AVE MOHAMED ZERKTOUNI
BOULEVARD MOULAY RACHID
Sefrou
POI
Information
Police Station
Airport
Railway Stn
Bus Station
Hospital

If you are driving into Fez, the Ville Nouvelle roads are open plan and easy to navigate. The Medina is ringed by Avenue Chefchaouen and is instantly visible by its ancient walls. Although cars can't drive within it, there are car parks beside most of the *babs* (city gates), such as Bou Jeloud and R'cif, as well as parking around Batha, Ziat and Ain Azliten.

FINDING YOUR FEET

While the modern Ville Nouvelle and the ramparts seem to operate to an easily understood rhythm, Fez's Medina is a law unto itself. That's its charm. However, it can be somewhat disorientating. Touts will try to coerce you into enlisting them as guides (this is now illegal in Fez); vendors will make you the focus of their hardest sell; overloaded donkeys and mules will

IF YOU GET LOST, TRY …

Excuse me, is this the right way to the tourist office/ the bus station?
Excusez-moi, c'est la bonne direction pour l'office de tourisme/la gare routière?
Ekskewzaymwah, seh lah bon deerekseeawng poor lohfeece de tooreezm/lah gahr rootyair?

Can you point to it on my map?
Pouvez-vous me le montrer sur la carte?
Poovehvoo mer ler mawngtreh sewr lah kart?

cause traffic jams and barge you out of the way. You'll probably need to find a corner and take a few breaths every once in a while.

Keep your possessions safe at all times and try not to wear expensive jewellery or carry much money or many valuables. Be wary of straying into deserted areas or the very tiny, empty alleyways without a guide. Places that are less visited and more impoverished (such as parts of the Al-Andalous and Fez el-Jdid areas) can be intimidating. Women may find they are less hassled in the Medina when they cover up. When you are with a guide (see below), you will receive no unwanted attention and this is the safest and most comfortable way of finding your feet.

ORIENTATION

Fez is notoriously difficult to navigate. Its Medina has some 9,000 streets, and to the first-time visitor it seems a miracle that even the longest-standing residents can get a handle on orientation. It cannot be stressed enough how useful it is to hire a guide on your initial forays – the layout of the Medina makes it a bewildering, and often alien, place at first. A guide will not only deter any extra hassle you get as an obvious tourist but show you the most important landmarks that act as pointers during your stay. Ask your hotel or *riad* to recommend an authorised guide.

The major sights are well marked in English, and there are also various recommended tourist trails that are marked out in pink, green and blue throughout the city. It's useful to remember Fez's Bou Jeloud Gate and the central arteries of Talaa Kebira and Talaa Seghira as landmarks. The area to the north is the best starting point, and easiest part to navigate, with wider streets and roads and a more open-plan layout. That said, the Medina's residents recognise the difficulties tourists face and will offer to help you – either out of goodwill or for a few dirham.

GETTING AROUND

The bus system is overcrowded. Taking a taxi is almost as cheap, and much more comfortable. There are two types: the small, red '*petits* taxis' do not travel beyond the centre; the big, champagne-coloured Mercedes, known as '*grands* taxis', go beyond the city borders and have several bases around town. Ask at your hotel for directions to the nearest one.

Both types of taxi are cheap, though be prepared to share. *Petits* taxis will pick up extra passengers en route while *grands* taxis don't leave until all six passenger spaces are filled. Taxi drivers normally use their meters, but if they don't, remind them or simply get out and take a different one.

As mentioned, fares are very cheap – it's rare that a *petit* taxi journey costs more than 20dh, even after 21.00 when fares rise by 30 per cent. Similarly, *grand* taxi fares rarely top 20dh for an hour's journey. However, travelling long distances with so many people in the heat can be stifling. It's also possible to pay for all six seats yourself and commandeer the whole vehicle; another top tip is to pay for two seats so that you occupy the entire front seat by yourself.

Over-laden donkeys can be a hazard when negotiating the narrow streets

TERRASE
LA MAISSON
DES TANNEURS

CAR HIRE

Car hire is relatively cheap in Fez, though you will still find taking taxis around the city more cost-effective. When exploring the out of town areas hiring a car is a wise idea, particularly if you're planning on making multiple stops. The lowest price for a day's car hire is around 350dh, inclusive of unlimited mileage and insurance, with a medium-sized car costing around double that.

Avis ⓐ 50 blvd Chefchaouen ⓣ (035) 62 69 69 ⓦ www.avis.ma
Budget ⓐ 6 av. Lalla Asma ⓣ (035) 594 00 92 ⓦ www.budget.com
Europcar ⓐ 45 av. Hassan II ⓣ (035) 562 65 45 ⓦ www.europcar.com
First Car ⓐ Av. des F.A.R ⓣ (035) 593 09 09 ⓦ www.firstcar.ma
Hertz ⓐ 1 av. Lalla Meryem ⓣ (035) 62 28 12 ⓦ www.hertz.com

Tower, gate and ramparts in the Al-Andalous district

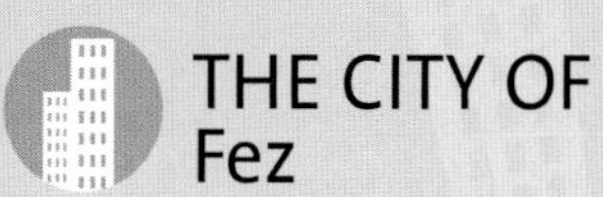

THE CITY OF Fez

The Medina

Arguably the key reason for visiting Fez, the Medina (formally – but rarely – known as Medina el-Bali) is a vivid labyrinth of 9,000 streets and alleyways containing some of the finest craftsmanship in the world, as well as Morocco's oldest and most holy sights. Founded in AD 789 by Moulay Idriss and designated a UNESCO World Heritage site in 1981, it is the country's largest *medina* and probably the world's most extensive urban car-free zone. This area has a rich past, but it's now poised to embrace the future. Upmarket boutiques, cafés and designer *riads* are now throwing open their doors alongside the historic buildings and monuments.

SIGHTS & ATTRACTIONS

Bab Bou Jeloud

Probably the city's most recognisable landmark, the stunning, gaping blue and white arch greeting those entering the Medina is a great starting-point for some serious exploration and a definite must-see. You'll probably wind your way back here quite a few times during your visit. ⓐ Northwest of Batha

Bou Inania Medersa

One of the few *medersas* (schools) that you can actually enter, this is one of the Medina's most exquisite finds. It is an exemplar of this type of organisation but is no longer functioning. ⓐ Talaa Kebira ⓑ 09.00–19.00. Admission charge

Bab Bou Jeloud is the gateway to the Medina

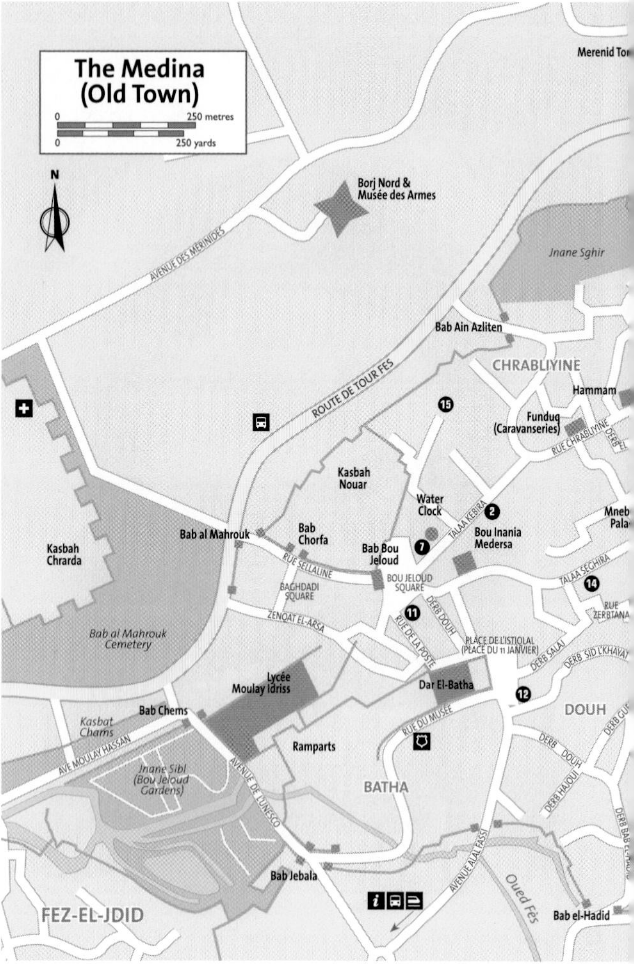

The Medina (Old Town)

0 250 metres
0 250 yards

N

Merenid Tombs
Borj Nord & Musée des Armes
AVENUE DES MERINIDES
Jnane Sghir
Bab Ain Azliten
CHRABLIYINE
ROUTE DE TOUR FES
Hammam
15
Funduq (Caravanseries)
RUE CHRABLIYINE
Kasbah Nouar
Water Clock
TALAA KEBIRA
2
Bou Inania Medersa
Bab al Mahrouk
Bab Chorfa
Bab Bou Jeloud
7
Kasbah Chrarda
RUE SELLALINE
BOU JELOUD SQUARE
BAGHDADI SQUARE
TALAA SEGHIRA
14
RUE ZERBTANA
11
ZENQAT EL-ARSA
DERB DOUH
RUE DE LA POSTE
Bab al Mahrouk Cemetery
PLACE DE L'ISTIQLAL (PLACE DU 11 JANVIER)
DERB SALAJ
DERB SIDI L'KHAYAT
Lycée Moulay Idriss
Dar El-Batha
12
DOUH
Bab Chems
RUE DU MUSÉE
Kasbat Chams
AVE MOULAY HASSAN
Ramparts
DERB DOUH
Jnane Sibl (Bou Jeloud Gardens)
AVENUE DE L'UNESCO
BATHA
DERB HAJOUI
AVENUE ALAL FASSI
Oued Fès
Bab Jebala
FEZ-EL-JDID
Bab el-Hadid

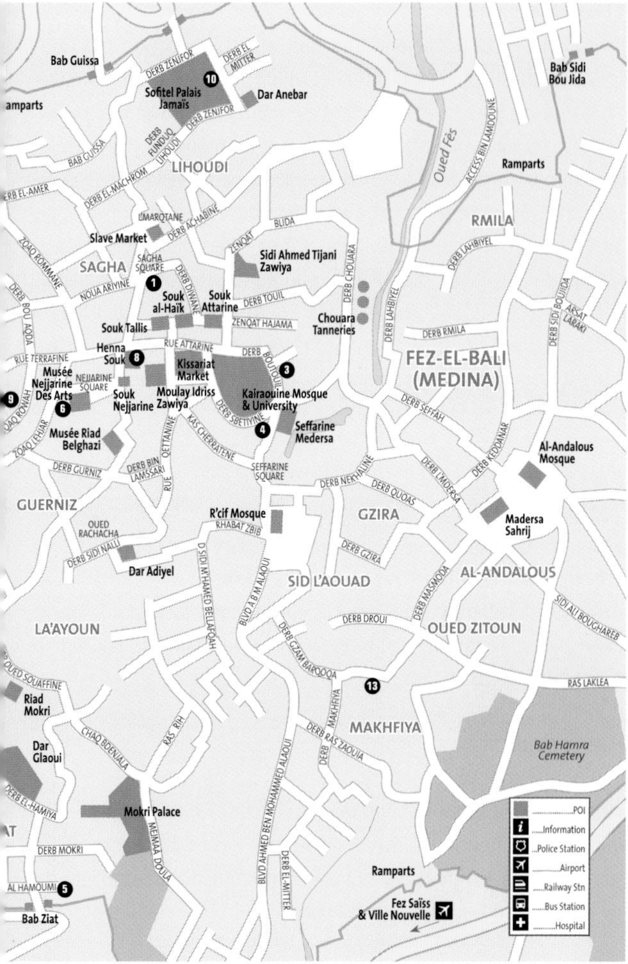

Bab Guissa
DERB ZENJFOR
DERB EL MITTER
Sofitel Palais Jamaïs
10
Dar Anebar
amparts
DERB ZENJFOR
DERB FUNDUQ
LIHOUDI
BAB GUISSA
DERB EL-MACHROM
LIHOUDI
ERB EL-AMER
L'MAROTANE
DERB ACHABINE
Slave Market
ZENQAT
BLIDA
Sidi Ahmed Tijani Zawiya
ZQAQ ROMMANE
SAGHA
SAGHA SQUARE
DERB DIWANE
1
NOUA ARIYINE
Souk al-Haïk
Souk Attarine
DERB TOUIL
DERB CHOUARA
DERB BOU AQDA
Souk Tallis
ZENQAT HAJAMA
Chouara Tanneries
RUE ATTARINE
RUE TERRAFINE
Henna Souk
8
Kissariat Market
DERB BOUTOUIL
3
Musée Nejjarine Des Arts
NEJJARINE SQUARE
Souk Nejjarine
Moulay Idriss Zawiya
Kairaouine Mosque & University
9
6
ZQAQ ROWAH
DERB SBETIYINE
4
KAS CHERRATENE
Seffarine Medersa
ZQAQ LEHJAR
Musée Riad Belghazi
RUE OETTANINE
DERB BIN LAMSSARI
DERB GURNIZ
SEFFARINE SQUARE
GUERNIZ
OUED RACHACHA
DERB SIDI NALLI
Dar Adiyel
R'cif Mosque
RHABAT ZBIB
D SIDI M'HAMED BELLAFOAH
BLVD A B M ALAOUI
SID L'AOUAD
Bab Sidi Bou Jida
Oued Fès
ACCESS BIN LAMDOUNE
Ramparts
RMILA
DERB LAHBIYEL
DERB LAHBIYEL
DERB SIDI BOUJIDA
ARSAT LARAKI
DERB RMILA
FEZ-EL-BALI (MEDINA)
DERB SEFFAH
DERB NEKHALINE
DERB QUOAS
DERB L'MDERSA
DERB KEDDANAR
Al-Andalous Mosque
GZIRA
DERB GZIRA
Madersa Sahrij
AL-ANDALOUS
DERB MASMODA
SIDI ALI BOUGHAREB
LA'AYOUN
DERB DROUI
OUED ZITOUN
DERB GZAM BAROOQA
OUED SOUAFFINE
13
RAS LAKLEA
Riad Mokri
DERB MAKHFIYA
MAKHFIYA
RAS RIH
CHAQ BDENJALA
DERB RAS ZAOUIA
Bab Hamra Cemetery
Dar Glaoui
DERB EL-HAMIYA
Mokri Palace
MEIMAA DOULA
BLVD AHMED BEN MOHAMMED ALAOUI
DERB EL-MITTER
AT
DERB MOKRI
Ramparts
AL HAMOUMI
5
Bab Ziat
Fez Saïss & Ville Nouvelle

POI
Information
Police Station
Airport
Railway Stn
Bus Station
Hospital

Chouara Tanneries

One of the most iconic and unforgettable sights in Fez can be found in these ancient tanneries, which were established in the 13th century and are still worked by some 10,000 tanners today. Their giant vats are emblazoned with the colours of the dyes – red from poppies, blue from indigo, green from wild mint, yellow from saffron, orange from henna and white from the limestone and pigeon excrement used to strip the hides of camels, goats, sheep and cows. Ask one of the vendors to talk you through the dyeing process. The vision is as lasting as the smell – so pungent that you'll need to grab a sprig of mint to mask it. If you're brave, ask the friendly tanners to show you around at ground level. ⓐ Derb Chouara ⓛ 08.00–18.00

Dar Glaoui

This beautiful abandoned palace belonging to the prestigious Glaoui family comprises 17 houses, a mausoleum, cemetery, harem, spa and stables. Although it has fallen into slight disrepair, it still provides one of the most captivating examples of regal Fassi architecture. ⓐ 1 Derb el-Hamiya, Ziat ⓣ (067) 36 68 28 ⓛ 10.00–19.00

Henna Souk

The oldest *souk* in Fez is a tiny opening off the streets surrounding Kairaouine. Today, pottery shops have largely replaced the henna stalls where women were once adorned for weddings. Inside is the old psychiatric hospital, established by the Merenids in the 13th century.

Observe the leather tanners at the ancient Chouara Tanneries

Kairaouine Mosque & University

The largest mosque in Africa was built in AD 859 and can hold some 20,000 worshippers. It has been magnificently restored. Its symmetrical white arches and pillars signify architectural genius, and the rolling courtyards are fringed by 14 entrances, the main one incorporating beautifully carved screens. It's well worth walking the full perimeter, from where you'll catch glimpses of the interiors as the faithful enter for prayer. The adjoining *medersa* is allegedly the oldest university in the world. ⓐ Near Seffarine Square

L'Marqtane

This square, near Sagha, is a former slave market where captives were sold in the open air. Auctions these days are for leather, and take place every day at 15.30. ⓐ Achebine, Sagha

Moulay Idriss Zawiya

The tomb of Moulay Idriss is set in the heart of the Medina. Observe the low bar at the entrance to the road leading to it: this was in place until 1912 as a symbolic means of keeping police, animals and non-believers away from such a holy site. Non-Muslims can't enter the shrine, but can see the exquisite cedar wood doors and witness the religious intensity as they approach.

Nejjarine Souk

Located to the right of Nejjarine Square, this is a covered carpenters' thoroughfare where the smell of freshly sawn wood pervades and the elaborate accoutrements of marriage are crafted and displayed for all to see.

Seffarine Square

One of the must-visits of Fez, this square at the helm of the brass-makers' *souk* has been compared to an orchestra pit – except that the instruments here are hammers, as they beat and shape the metal on the steps of the square. Here you'll also find the Seffarine Medersa (the first to be built by the Merenids, in 1270) with its courtyard pool.

Sidi Ahmed Tijani Zawiya

Located close to the Kairaouine Mosque (see left) is the second most important mausoleum in Fez. It is visited by devotees from all over North Africa, though non-Muslims can only glimpse it through the open door.

Visit the Batha Museum for an inight into Fassi history

Water Clock

It is thought that the 13 wooden blocks that lie beneath the windows of this 14th-century house held water bowls that somehow operated as a clock. Allegedly created by a magician, no-one has ever quite determined how it worked. ⓐ Talaa Kebira, opposite Bou Inania

CULTURE

Dar Adiyel

This lovely old *medersa* has a cool courtyard and is home to Fez's musicians. Every day at 15.00 between Monday and Thursday, music students perform free concerts. ⓐ Oued Rachacha, Derb Sidi Nalli ⓛ 09.00–18.00. Admission charge

Dar El-Batha (Batha Museum)

Fez's largest museum is situated in a grand summer palace. It exhibits a fascinating collection of historic Fassi objects, Berber jewellery and artefacts and relics from the city's past. The building is fringed by a beautiful courtyard garden. ⓐ Rue du Musée, Place de l'Istiqlal ⓣ (035) 63 41 16 ⓛ 08.00–12.00, 14.30–18.00 Wed–Mon. Admission charge

Musée Nejjarine des Arts

One of Fez's most popular museums is set within an enchanting square. The building, a former VIP *funduq* (a hotel where travellers had space to stable their horses at ground level), is a work of art in itself and has been exquisitely restored by UNESCO. Dating back to the tenth century and with the most intricate mosaics

Inside Dar Adiyel – the music school

and cedar carvings outside and within, the building's foyer contains huge scales. Upstairs the museum is a showcase of all things Fassi – from intricately carved screens and tiny marriage chairs for child brides to Berber furniture and shrine-coverings set across three enchanting floors. ⓐ Nejjarine Square ⓛ 09.00–19.00. Admission charge

Musée Riad Belghazi

This sprawling *riad* museum showcases heritage items from the area. Berber and Arabic artefacts encompass ancient manuscripts, weapons and cultural mementos such as wedding gowns, daggers, shrine coverings and 18th-century musical instruments. The building is a fine example of a *riad*. You can take tea in the courtyard. ⓐ 19 Dab el-Ghorba, Guerniz ⓣ (064) 50 94 59 ⓛ 09.00–18.30. Admission charge

Riad Mokri

The dilapidated ruins of this former palace of the powerful Mokri family host regular concerts, and the multi-tiered lawns boast unrivalled views of the Medina and the Middle Atlas beyond. Even when there is no music, Mokri offers a sweet spot to poke your head in and gaze at the views. ⓐ Oued Souaffine ⓣ (068) 60 17 91 ⓦ www.lesmusicalesdefes.com ⓛ Opening times vary – check website for details. Admission charge

RETAIL THERAPY

Arganza An upmarket boutique selling all things made from argan oil, from giant candles and cooking oil to anti-ageing cosmetic lotions. ⓐ 9 rue de la Poste, Batha ⓣ (035) 63 86 56 ⓦ www.arganzaoil.com ⓗ 10.00–20.00 Sat–Thur

Bella Casa A magnet for magpies, this fantastic shop purveys every kind of sparkling bangle you could dream of, in every colour and size under the sun. Chic belly-dancer outfits dazzle further still. ⓐ 19 Zqaq Lehjar, Talaa Seghira ⓣ (014) 18 88 60 ⓦ www.fesdecoration.com ⓗ 09.00–21.00

Chez La Famille Berbère This lovely shop is chock full of curiosities, from intricate metalware to ceramics, jewellery and furniture. It's one of the most popular stops on the Talaa Kebira tourist trail and its location just off the main artery makes browsing a pleasure. ⓐ 27 Ras Tayaline, off Talaa Kebira ⓣ (035) 74 12 29 ⓗ 09.00–21.00

Coine de Henne Abdou's Berber herbal medicine and spice shop is timewarp stuff. Almost Victorian in appearance, it brims with potions, tonics and tinctures designed to salve every last complaint, from herbal Viagra to stress relievers and anti-ageing creams. ⓐ 148 Sidi Moussa, Guerniz ⓣ (035) 63 81 27 ⓗ 10.00–20.00 Sat–Thur

Fès Art Gallery This vast, ornate *riad* has original fountains, intricate painted screens and urns alongside a selection of jewellery across a number of tiers. The terrace at the top of the shop boasts probably the best views non-Muslims will glimpse of the Kairaouine Mosque and University. ⓐ 2 Boutouil, Kairaouine ⓣ (035) 63 46 63 ⓗ 09.30–19.30 Sat–Thur; 09.30–13.00 Fri

SOUKS OF THE MEDINA

Whether you're perusing for presents or pleasure, the *souks* are among the Medina's greatest attractions. Here's a guide to the best:

Achebine Souk This fascinating *souk* is situated off L'Marqtane, and houses the food stalls from which locals buy their lunches.

Dyers' Souk This short, wide alley houses the dyers' quarter, which feels like it's barely changed since the tenth century. Experts plunge fabrics into vast bubbling vats and hang the garments out to dry.

Funduq Kaat Smen This little fresh produce market tucked off the main artery is where locals come to stock up on honey, olive oil and argan oil.

Henna Souk This open-air courtyard is the oldest *souk* in the Medina and contains an array of shops selling the blue-and-white pottery for which Fez is renowned.

Kissariat The large *kissariat* is a hustling, bustling hive of activity under one huge ceiling where you'll find all manner of embroidered *jellabas*, *babouches* and a few jewellery stalls.

Nejjarine Quarter and Square The square is a great place for picking up knick-knacks. Beside it a covered passage houses the carpenters' *souk*.

Quartier Des Tanneurs Here you can pick up an array of good quality leather – from jackets to briefcases and wallets in a variety of hand-stitched colours and styles.

Seffarine Quarter Famous for its brassware, this is a fascinating area bordering Seffarine Square.
Souk Attarine One of Fez's most memorable *souks*, this primarily sells spices and perfumes, but along the way you'll spy animals, tinctures and potions.
Souk Bab Bou Jeloud A fruit and veg market where you'll also see chickens clucking alongside more unusual buys such as live hedgehogs and camels' heads.

Check out the metalwork in Seffarine Square

There's a cure for everything in this spice and herbal medicine shop

Fez Shop If someone at home begs you to bring them back one of the eponymous hats, check out this hole-in-the-wall specialist shop that looks like it hasn't changed since it was opened by the owner's father in 1958. Purveying some of the finest fezzes in Fez, there are old-school pictures of the founder modelling his wares. ⓐ 127 rue Qettanine ⓣ (035) 06 12 65 ◷ 10.00–13.00, 15.00–20.00

L'Art Traditionnel A panoply of beautiful brass objects is sold in this lovely shop in an upmarket lane – the owner's family have been crafting the stunning pierced brass lanterns, some inlaid with exquisitely coloured intricate glasswork, for generations. ⓐ 8 Derb Boutouil ⓣ (035) 63 57 69 ◷ 09.00–20.00 Sat–Thur, 09.00–12.00 Fri

Les Mystères de Fès More like a *riad* museum than a shop, the renowned collection of antiques and *objets d'art* in this gallery make it every inch an Aladdin's cave. ⓐ 53 Derb bin Lemssari, Sidi Moussa ⓣ (035) 63 61 48 ◷ 09.00–19.00 Sat–Thur

Made in M A trendy and welcoming boutique purveying items of new Moroccan craft such as chic leather holdalls and some rather attractive lights. ⓐ 246 Talaa Kebira ⓣ (011) 05 48 63 ◷ 09.00–20.00 Sat–Thur

Maison de Bronze A gleaming collection of antique and contemporary jewellery, arms and *objets d'art* can be found in this vast emporium that sells all things bronze and silver. ⓐ 3 Derb el-Horra ⓣ (061) 28 03 11 ◷ 08.30–19.00

Maison des Brodeuses Fassies Tucked away down a side street, this workshop-cum-gift-shop showcases the finest Fassi sewing. The seamstresses stitch before your eyes. ⓐ 50 Derb Beni Aich, Talaa Seghira ⓣ (035) 63 33 30 ⓛ 09.00–19.00

Palais des Babouches A funky array of the leather shoes (or *babouches*) native to Morocco goes above and beyond what you'll find in the more traditional outposts. The shop has up-to-the-minute styles as well as charming giant *babouche* holdalls. ⓐ 36/3 Zqaq Lehjar, Talaa Seghira ⓣ (035) 77 28 66 ⓛ 10.00–21.00 Sat–Thur

Tonnelier Mohammed Tazi sits on his bed of sawdust in this hole-in-the-wall within one of the Medina's main streets, crafting classic beechwood buckets with gilt belts for the *hammams* by hand. ⓐ 53 rue Chrabliyine, Talaa Kebira ⓣ (035) 60 54 16 ⓛ 09.00–19.00 Sat–Thur

TAKING A BREAK

Café Ba Bouchta £ ❶ Set within Fez's oldest bank, this local haunt has the usual array of Fassi suspects drinking mint tea or coffee. You can look over the street below via the engraved wall that surrounds the café, and get a glimpse of the age-old practice of heating water over a fire. ⓐ Old Bank, 33 Sagha Square ⓛ 06.00–22.00

Café Berbère £ ❷ The ebullient character who runs this psychedelic, Berber-themed sliver of a café likes to impress his heritage upon guests. Steaming mint tea is the order of the day, but the main draw is watching the foot soldiers of the Talaa Kebira bustle past. ⓐ 66 Talaa Kebira ⓣ (070) 99 75 96 ⓛ 09.00–22.00

Café Kourtobe £ ❸ A pillar of the Fassi café scene that has been going for 200 years. Wonderfully old school and friendly, it's little more than a hole in the heaving Kairaouine artery. Sample a delicious cake, homemade ice-cream or milkshake with coffee and orange juice around shared tables. ⓐ 11–13 Derb Boutouil, Kairaouine ⓛ 07.00–22.00

Cremerie La Place £ ❹ This neat little spot slap bang on Seffarine Square has two tables in pole position outside. Selling mint tea, coffee and freshly squeezed orange juice, it's a great spot from which to observe the world going by. ⓐ 14 Seffarine Square ⓣ (070) 99 75 96 ⓛ 08.00–20.30 Sat–Thur, 08.00–00.00 Fri

Fès & Gestes £ ❺ Opened in summer 2008 as part of the new wave of upmarket bohemian hangouts, this chic, French-run tearoom is a picturesque place to take a break over a pot of green tea or herbal infusion. Equally, you can savour the set two-course lunch in the garden. ⓐ 39 Rasat el-Hamoumi, Ziat ⓣ (035) 63 85 32 ⓛ 09.00–19.00 Thur–Tues

Musée Nejjarine des Arts Café £ ❻ You'll have to enter via the museum, but once up top you won't be disappointed. With views over the Medina and a quiet environment in which to sip a mint tea or something cooler, you might even see hens strutting about here. ⓐ Nejjarine Square ⓛ 10.00–19.00

Café Clock ££ ❼ One of the top spots in which to grab a bite to eat in the Medina, this English-owned café-cum-arts-outpost is tucked away behind the main street. The building is a converted 17th-century *riad* covering four floors, with a sprawling roof terrace overlooking one of the most captivating *medersa* minarets. With a programme of live events, from henna painting to concerts and from rotating art exhibitions to calligraphy courses, there's great, friendly service, Wi-Fi internet access, a library and good, wholesome food – don't miss the camel burgers or the signature lemon tart. ⓐ 7 Derb el-Margana, Talaa Kebira ⓣ (035) 63 78 55 ⓦ www.cafeclock.com ◷ 09.00–22.00

Dar Saada ££ ❽ One of the grand *riad* restaurants in which to sample impeccable Fassi service and multiple-course cuisine, taking in delights such as decadent *pastillas* and ginger and strawberry chicken *tagines*. Make sure you get a seat facing the front door, so that you can witness the theatre of both the restaurant and the spice market beyond simultaneously. ⓐ 21 rue Attarine ⓣ (035) 63 73 70 ⓦ www.restaurantdarsaada.com ◷ 12.00–16.00, 19.30–22.30

F Lounge ££ ❾ Chic, upmarket Spanish-run restaurant-cum-lounge with comfortable seating and positively 21st-century design. This more recent addition to the style spectrum serves soups, paninis and caviar alongside Italian specialities and *shisha* pipes. ⓐ 95 Derb Zqaq Rowah ⓣ (014) 19 94 40 ◷ 11.00–21.00

L'Oliveraie ££ ❿ A superior spot in which to escape the heat of the Medina and revel in the glorious views over the city. The

Enjoy a variety of entertainment at Café Clock

Mediterranean buffet and barbecues allow you to eat as much as you like and diners are given access to the swimming pool and loungers of the hotel. The terrace here also offers one of the finest spots to take in the sunset over the Medina. ⓐ Sofitel Palais Jamaï, Bab Guissa ⓣ (035) 63 43 31 ⓛ 08.00–00.00

AFTER DARK

RESTAURANTS

Restaurant la Kasbah £ ⑪ Few vantage points can compare to that of this Fez institution, seated high up on the terraces overlooking the Bou Jeloud gates. Perennially popular with tourists, its menu serves up no-nonsense Moroccan grub at a money-saving 70dh for three courses. ⓐ 10 Serrafine, near Bab Bou Jeloud ⓣ (035) 74 15 33 ⓛ 20.00–23.00

La Maison Bleue £££ ⑫ A textbook example of Fassi cuisine and hospitality set in the environment of Fez's oldest hotel. Your name is spelt out in petals on the table and a four-course supper incorporates a panoply of salads served in baby *tagines*. ⓐ 2 pl. de l'Istiqlal ⓣ (035) 74 18 43 ⓦ www.maisonbleue.com ⓛ 11.00–00.00

Palais de Fès £££ ⑬ Entry is through an old carpet shop and the sprawling terrace on which you eat offers one of the best views over the Medina. The traditional cuisine is terrific. ⓐ 15 Makhfiya ⓣ (055) 76 15 90 ⓦ www.palaisdefes.com ⓛ 11.00–00.00

Riad Fès £££ ⑭ Slick service, sophisticated fashionable surrounds and an ambience that instantly seduces. Here you can enjoy local *haute cuisine* such as prawns in homemade sauce and semolina-stuffed chicken, pigeon and ginger beef in the charming courtyard surroundings. ⓐ Derb ben Slimane, Zerbtana ⓣ (035) 94 76 10 ⓦ www.riadfes.com ⓛ 08.00–23.00

Ryad Mabrouka £££ ⓯ You'll have to give 24 hours' notice for a chance of getting a table at this hidden gem. The food is top-notch, with an international menu available upon request alongside traditional Moroccan fare, produced by a chef who has served time at some of the world's leading hotels. ⓐ Derb el-Mitter, Ain Azliten ⓣ (035) 63 63 45 ⓛ 19.30–22.00

BARS

L'Alcazar Probably the Medina's most sophisticated drinking spot, where Ibiza-style sounds dominate against a backdrop of cocktails and designer threads around the courtyard pool at Riad Fès. ⓐ Derb ben Slimane, Zerbtana ⓣ (035) 94 76 10 ⓦ www.riadfes.com ⓛ 20.00–00.00

Hotel Batha With the only pub in the Medina – if not Fez itself – the Hotel Batha is a long-established drinking spot. The atmosphere very much depends on the crowd. ⓐ Pl. de L'Istiqlal ⓣ (035) 63 48 24 ⓛ 10.00–01.00

Sofitel Palais Jamaï ££ One of the best places to sip a beverage and view the sun setting over the Medina is the terrace at the veteran Palais Jamaï. There's also a somewhat subdued bar within the hotel itself. ⓐ Bab Guissa ⓣ (035) 63 43 31 ⓛ 08.00–00.00

Al-Andalous, el-Jdid & the Ramparts

Al-Andalous is the oldest part of the Medina, named after Andalucia, in Spain, from where its founders had come. The ramparts gradually developed as fortifications for the old city, defending it against foreign invaders. Today a wealth of diversions peppers the surroundings of the Medina, from luxury bars and iconic monuments to hustling, thriving potteries and Fez el-Jdid. Edgier, more run-down and home-grown than its neighbour, the Medina, it's worth taking a walk down to el-Jdid if only to gain an idea of the rougher, more authentic side of Fez. Other attractions are the fascinating Mellah, now abandoned by Morocco's Jewish community but still worth a hop over the city walls, and the Royal Palace with its grand golden doors. All of these are presided over by the Borj Sud and old Merenid Tombs.

SIGHTS & ATTRACTIONS

Al-Andalous Mosque

Fez's most ancient mosque is to the Andalous area what the Kairaouine (see page 66) is to the Medina. The mosque dominates the least touristic section of the old town and forms the hub of its thoroughfares and its entire religious aspect. It has all the signature hallmarks of sculpture, intricacy and calm. Only Muslims who have come to worship at times of prayer may enter the Mosque.

Alaouites Square & Royal Palace

This princely, gleaming square with manicured shrubbery that

Grand entrance to the Royal Palace

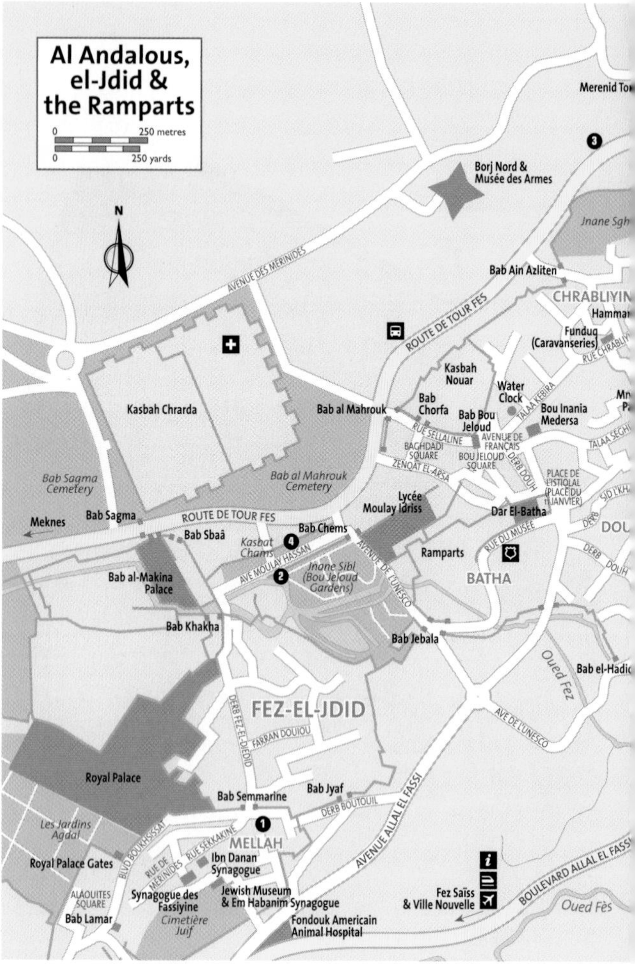

Al Andalous, el-Jdid & the Ramparts

0 250 metres
0 250 yards

N

Merenid To
Borj Nord & Musée des Armes
Jnane Sgh
AVENUE DES MERINIDES
Bab Ain Azliten
CHRABLIYIN
Hamma
ROUTE DE TOUR FES
Funduq (Caravanseries)
RUE CHRABLIY
Kasbah Nouar
Water Clock
TALAA KEBIRA
Mn
P
Kasbah Chrarda
Bab al Mahrouk
Bab Chorfa
Bab Bou Jeloud
Bou Inania Medersa
TALAA SEGHI
RUE SELLALINE
AVENUE DE FRANÇAIS
BAGHDADI SQUARE
BOU JELOUD SQUARE
DERB DOUH
ZENQAT EL-ARSA
PLACE DE L'ISTIQLAL (PLACE DU 11 JANVIER)
SIDI L'KH
Bab Sagma Cemetery
Bab al Mahrouk Cemetery
Lycée Moulay Idriss
Dar El-Batha
Mekness
Bab Sagma
ROUTE DE TOUR FES
Bab Chems
DERB
DOU
Bab Sbaâ
Kasbat Chams
RUE DU MUSÉE
AVE MOULAY HASSAN
AVENUE DE L'UNESCO
Ramparts
DERB DOUH
Bab al-Makina Palace
Jnane Sibl (Bou Jeloud Gardens)
BATHA
Bab Khakha
Bab Jebala
Oued Fez
Bab el-Hadi
FEZ-EL-JDID
DERB FEZ-EL-DJEDID
FARRAN DOUIOU
AVE DE L'UNESCO
Royal Palace
Bab Jyaf
Bab Semmarine
DERB BOUTOUIL
AVENUE ALLAL EL FASSI
Les Jardins Agdal
BLVD BOUKHSISSAT
RUE SEKKAKINE
MELLAH
RUE DE MERINIDES
Royal Palace Gates
Ibn Danan Synagogue
BOULEVARD ALLAL EL FASSI
ALAOUITES SQUARE
Synagogue des Fassiyine
Jewish Museum & Em Habanim Synagogue
Fez Saïss & Ville Nouvelle
Oued Fès
Bab Lamar
Cimetière Juif
Fondouk Americain Animal Hospital

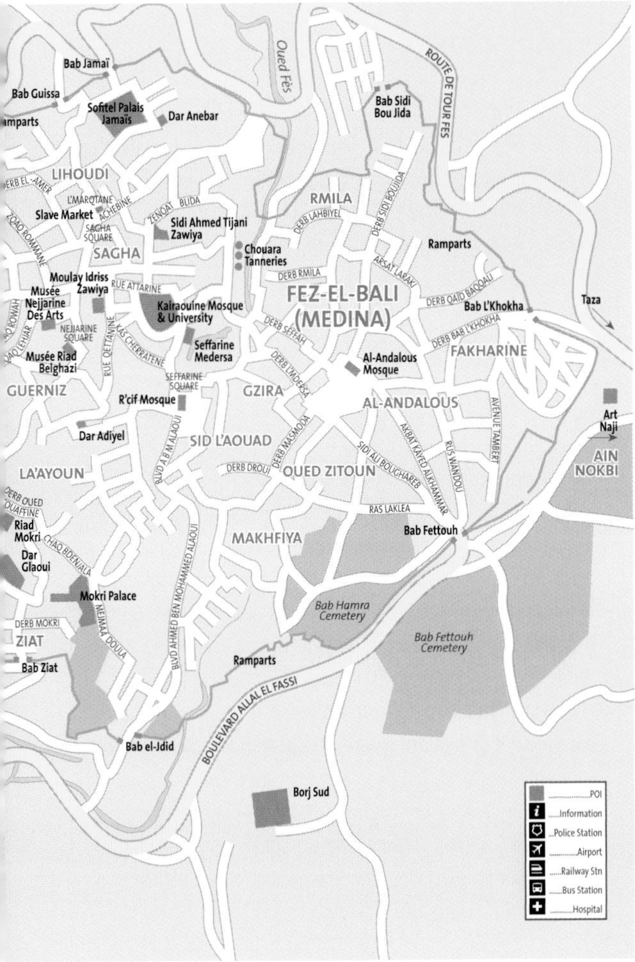

Bab Jamaï
Bab Guissa
Sofitel Palais Jamaïs
Dar Anebar
Ramparts
Oued Fès
ROUTE DE TOUR FES
Bab Sidi Bou Jida
LIHOUDI
DERB EL-AMER
L'MARQTANE
ACHEBINE
Slave Market
ZENQAT BLIDA
SAGHA SQUARE
SAGHA
ZQAQ ROMMANE
Sidi Ahmed Tijani Zawiya
Chouara Tanneries
RMILA
DERB LAHBIYEL
DERB SIDI BOUJIDA
Ramparts
ARSAT LARAKI
DERB RMILA
Moulay Idriss Zawiya
RUE ATTARINE
Musée Nejjarine Des Arts
NEJJARINE SQUARE
ZQAQ ROWAH
ZQAQ LEHJAR
Kairaouine Mosque & University
FEZ-EL-BALI (MEDINA)
DERB QAID BAQQALI
Bab L'Khokha
Taza
DERB BAB L'KHOKHA
DERB SEFFAH
RUE OETTANINE
KAS CHERRATENE
Seffarine Medersa
Musée Riad Belghazi
DERB L'MEDERSA
FAKHARINE
Al-Andalous Mosque
SEFFARINE SQUARE
GUERNIZ
R'cif Mosque
GZIRA
AL-ANDALOUS
Art Naji
AVENUE TAMBERT
Dar Adiyel
BLVD A B M ALAOUI
SID L'AOUAD
DERB MASMODA
SIDI ALI BOUGHAREB
AKBAT KAYED ALKHAMMAR
RUS WANDOU
AIN NOKBI
LA'AYOUN
DERB DROUJ
OUED ZITOUN
DERB OUED SOUAFFINE
RAS LAKLEA
Riad Mokri
CHAQ BDENJALA
MAKHFIYA
Bab Fettouh
Dar Glaoui
BLVD AHMED BEN MOHAMMED ALAOUI
Mokri Palace
MEIMAA DOULA
Bab Hamra Cemetery
DERB MOKRI
ZIAT
Bab Fettouh Cemetery
Bab Ziat
Ramparts
BOULEVARD ALLAL EL FASSI
Bab el-Jdid
Borj Sud

■	......POI
i	......Information
	...Police Station
	......Airport
	......Railway Stn
	......Bus Station
+	......Hospital

MOROCCO'S JEWS

Jews and Moroccans have a powerful and intertwined past. It's thought that the first Jewish settlers arrived in AD 70, at a time when the land was solely inhabited by Berbers, with whom they developed a harmonious relationship.

However, when Moulay Idriss I arrived, bringing with him the powerful message of Islam, nearly all Berbers converted and the Jews largely hid, for fear of reprisal if they did not convert. When the more tolerant Moulay Idriss II succeeded to the throne, the Jews were invited to settle in his capital, Fez.

The subsequent Merenid dynasty created the Mellah (see page 88) as a residential area for Jews, and Fassi Jews were soon joined by their cousins fleeing the inquisition in Spain. Many rose to positions of considerable power, installed as ambassadors in foreign courts under the reign of Moulay Ismail (1672–1727), who chose several as his closest consorts. Moroccans and Jews lived together in harmony for hundreds of years. In the 20th century, when King Mohammed V was asked by the Nazis to extradite his Jews, he refused to do so, claiming that everyone in his country was a Moroccan. Although the Jewish population of Morocco has dwindled, with many of its members having emigrated to Israel, Jews still hold prominent positions in Moroccan government today. Morocco is considered Israel's closest ally in the Arab world, alongside Egypt.

seems to stretch on forever is strangely at odds with the neighbouring run-down Fez el-Jdid. It's the entrance to the largest and oldest palace in Morocco, bordered by two huge, gleaming golden gates. Like all palaces in Morocco, it's not possible to get any closer than the gates; the stately entrance and roaming walls, however, give you a taste of the beauty that must lie within. ⓐ Off blvd Boukhsissat

Fondouk Americain Animal Hospital
A must for animal lovers, this charitable veterinary hospital was established in 1927 by Amy Bend Bishop who had become alarmed by the lack of care provided to Morocco's working animals. Today the in-house vet, blacksmith and eight other staff tend to between 50 and 100 animals a day. It's located on the left hand side of the road down the hill from Fez el-Jdid. ⓐ Route de Taza ⓣ (035) 93 19 53 ⓦ www.fondouk.org Ⓛ 07.30–13.00

Ibn Danan Synagogue
This fascinating slice of the past was once the synagogue of the Mellah's Jewish congregation. The prayer room still has the original *torahs*, in addition to a photo exhibition about Morocco's Jews. Upstairs, the sprawling roof terrace offers views over the cemetery and synagogue. Down in the cellar is the original well, or *mikveh*, in which women ceremonially washed once a month for purification. ⓐ Rue de Djaj, off rue des Mérinides Ⓛ 07.00–19.00

Jnane Sbil (Bou Jeloud Gardens)
Here is where Fassis head to take a break and some shade. These pretty gardens line the old walls just beyond the Bou Jeloud area

of the Medina and border Fez el-Jdid. The Oued Fès flows through them, and they're peppered with fragrant myrtle, pomegranate and orange trees. ⓐ South of av. des Français ⓛ Dawn–dusk

Mellah

The houses of the former Jewish area with their lovely Romeo and Juliet-style balconies were established in the 13th century by the Merenids for Fez's growing community of Jews. The buildings lie parallel to the road between Alaouites and Fez el-Jdid (Boulevard Boukhsissat). These days the dwindling Jewish contingent has decamped to the Ville Nouvelle, but you can still look up in awe at the architecture.

Merenid Tombs

The vast, ancient ruins of the tombs of the mighty Merenid family date from the 14th century and dominate the skyline, lining a bank overlooking the Medina next to Borj Sud. They're a joy to wander through. At the bottom of the hill are some caves where people still live. ⓐ Av. des Mérinides

CULTURE

Art Naji

First the smoke hits you, then the smell. So much industry goes on at Fez's famous potteries, built along the ramparts, that a smog of black smoke hovers over the district. Inside, you can both see how the pottery is made and buy the wares at knockdown prices. ⓐ Ain Nokbi ⓣ (035) 66 91 66 ⓦ www.artnaji.net ⓛ 08.00-18.00

Ruins of the Merenid Tombs

Borj Nord & Musée des Armes

Built in the 16th century by the Saadian family, this imposing fortress presides over the banks of the Medina, the perfect vantage point from which to survey the sweeping stage for the bustling scenery below. It houses an idiosyncratic armoury museum and a giant cannon, once used to fight the Portuguese in the Battle of the Three Kings. ☎ (035) 64 75 66 ⏲ 09.00–16.00 Tue–Sun. Admission charge

Borj Sud

This impressive former fortress predates its sibling on the opposite bank, and has an even older artillery museum. It is the perfect vantage point from which to survey the beauty of the Medina and a reminder of times when people were prepared to fight over this beautiful city.

Graves at the Jewish Cemetery

Cimetière Juif & Synagogue
This sprawling, white cemetery that fringes the Mellah has a tiny UNESCO-backed synagogue museum to the south of its grounds. It explains the history and culture of Morocco's Jewry with an array of Semitic artefacts and memorabilia. ● 07.30–19.30. Admission charge

RETAIL THERAPY

Derb Fez el-Jdid
The *jellaba* section lying to the left of the *souk* when you enter from the gates at Fez el-Jdid has among the liveliest arrays of the floor-length embroidered garments to be found in Fez.

Rue Sekkakine
Another relic of the area's Jewish past, there is still a jewellery *souk* at the top of the Mellah, selling exquisite gold and gemstone-laden pieces at favourable prices.

TAKING A BREAK

Café Ourika £ ❶ Set on the main street, a little further on from the Mellah and the turning to Fez el-Jdid, this café won't be winning any design awards but it's among the few tenable spots for tourists to take a break. ⓐ Blvd Boukhsissat ● Opening hours vary

Restaurant la Noria £ ❷ This charming hidden gem in a byway off the Jnane Sbil sits in a pretty courtyard with a working

waterwheel and serves great chicken *tagine*. ⓐ 43 Derb Batna ⓣ (072) 42 16 99 ⓛ 07.00–21.30

AFTER DARK

RESTAURANTS

Hôtel les Mérinides ££ ❸ Overlooking the Medina, Mérinides has a vast terrace complete with generous leather seating and a good selection of alcoholic drinks. ⓐ Borj Nord ⓣ (035) 64 52 26 ⓛ 20.30–23.30

Mezzanine ££ ❹ Fez's first Western-influenced style bar spans three storeys and a roof terrace on the little street facing the Jnane Sbil. From the trendy Riad Fez stable, this is where in the-know visitors and chic Fassis head for an evening of sophisticated tapas, electronic music and deftly-mixed cocktails (a rare spot where you can drink a Mojito or Champagne that's not in a hotel). One of the city's trendiest destinations, and a blessed relief for those seeking upmarket clubbing. ⓐ 17 Kasbat Chams ⓣ (011) 07 83 36 ⓛ 11.00–01.00

ENTERTAINMENT

Son et Lumière Show This sound and light extravaganza presents Fez's history in a 45-minute show beneath the stars. The spectacle takes place Monday to Saturday evenings by the Borj Sud (see page 90). It's presented in four different languages depending on the night, so check with the tourist office in advance. ⓐ Borj Sud ⓛ Show starts 21.30 Mon–Sat, Mar–Oct

Check out the various levels at trendy Mezzanine

Ville Nouvelle

The sprawling Ville Nouvelle is the true face of Fassi modernity, quite a contrast with the Medina and its traditional ways. Established by the French in 1922, this is an area of wide, open boulevards, containing some of the city's main practical amenities and a cosmopolitan selection of restaurants. It is also the primary nightlife hub for the city's young. Until now, the Ville Nouvelle has not been a favourite destination among tourists, who find more interest in the Medina. That looks set to change, however, with the official *Projet Touristique* that aims to put the new part of town on every visitor's map. Between the Jnane Palace and the edge of the Medina a newly hip area is opening up, far removed from the fusty feel of the area's main street Avenue Hassan II. Here you'll find a wealth of chic cafés, shops and spas.

CULTURE

Complexe Culturel Al Houria
The brains behind some of the most important arts events in Fez, Al Houria assembles exhibitions, concerts, literary talks, and theatre and dance shows in the main performance venue of the city. ⓐ Av. Palestine ⓣ (035) 94 44 67 ⓦ www.fes-culture.ma ⓑ 08.30–12.15, 14.30–18.30 Mon–Fri

Institut Français de Fès
With a rolling programme of theatre, concerts and film screenings, this French institution is one of Fez's premier arts outposts, showcasing everything from fringe films to African

Manicured gardens run down the centre of palm-lined Avenue Hassan II

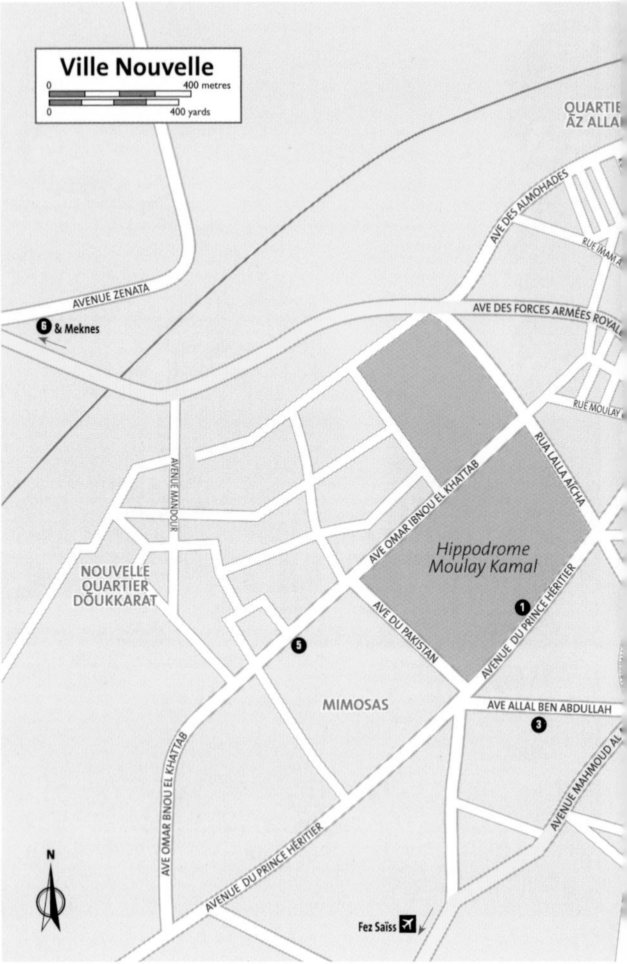

Ville Nouvelle

0 400 metres
0 400 yards

QUARTIE
ÂZ ALLA
AVE DES ALMOHADES
RUE IMAM A
AVENUE ZENATA
AVE DES FORCES ARMÉES ROYAL
6 & Meknes
RUE MOULAY
AVENUE MANDOUR
RUA LALLA AÏCHA
AVE OMAR IBNOU EL KHATTAB
Hippodrome Moulay Kamal
NOUVELLE QUARTIER DÔUKKARAT
AVENUE DU PRINCE HÉRITIER
1
AVE DU PAKISTAN
5
MIMOSAS
AVE ALLAL BEN ABDULLAH
3
AVENUE MAHMOUD AL
AVE OMAR BNOU EL KHATTAB
AVENUE DU PRINCE HÉRITIER
N
Fez Saïss

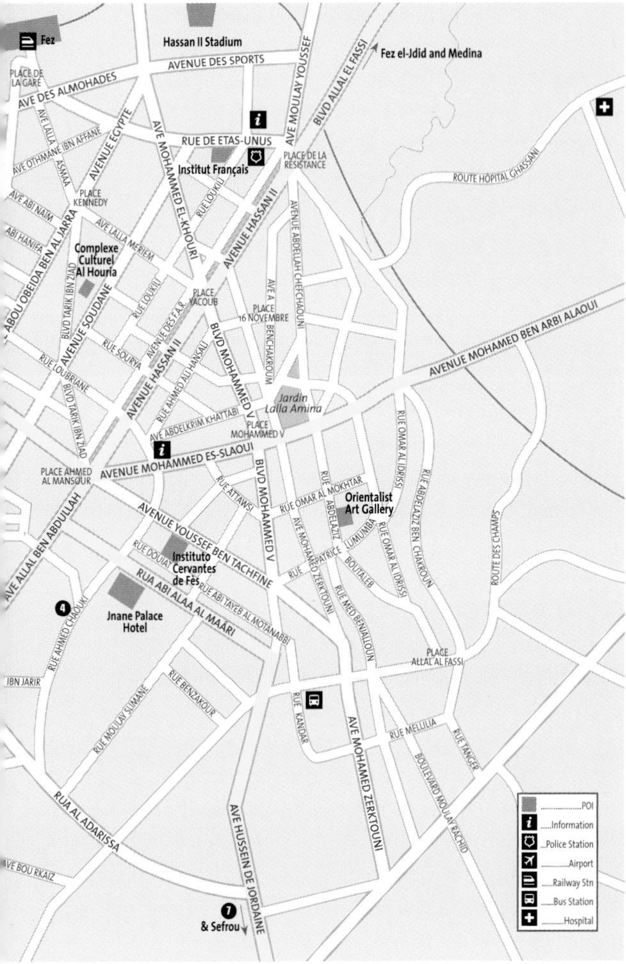

Fez
Hassan II Stadium
AVENUE DES SPORTS
Fez el-Jdid and Medina
PLACE DE LA GARE
AVE DES ALMOHADES
AVE LALLA ASMAA
AVE OTHMANE IBN AFFANE
AVENUE EGYPTE
AVE MOHAMMED EL-KHOURI
RUE DE ETAS-UNUS
AVE MOULAY YOUSSEF
BLVD ALLAL EL FASSI
Institut Français
PLACE DE LA RESISTANCE
ROUTE HOPITAL GHASSANI
PLACE KENNEDY
AVE ABI NAIM
ABI HANIFA
AVE LALLA MERIEM
RUE LOUKILI
AVENUE HASSAN II
AVENUE ABDELLAH CHEFCHAOUNI
ABOU OBEIDA BEN AL JARRA
Complexe Culturel Al Houria
BLVD TARIK IBN ZIAD
AVENUE SOUDANE
PLACE YACOUB
AVENUE DES F.A.R.
PLACE 16 NOVEMBRE
AVE A. BENCHAKROUM
BLVD MOHAMMED V
RUE SOURYA
RUE AHMED ALI HANSALI
RUE LOUBRIANE
AVENUE MOHAMED BEN ARBI ALAOUI
Jardin Lalla Amina
RUE ABDELKRIM KHATTABI
PLACE MOHAMMED V
AVENUE MOHAMMED ES-SLAOUI
PLACE AHMED AL MANSOUR
RUE OMAR AL IDRISSI
RUE ABDELAZIZ BEN CHAKROUN
RUE ATTAWSI
RUE OMAR AL MOKHTAR
Orientalist Art Gallery
AVE ALLAL BEN ABDULLAH
AVENUE YOUSSEF BEN TACHFINE
RUE DOUIAT
Instituto Cervantes de Fès
RUE ABDELAZIZ
RUE LUMUMBA
RUE PATRICE
AVE MOHAMED ZERKTOUNI
RUE BOUTALEB
ROUTE DES CHAMPS
RUE ABI TAYEB AL MOTANABBI
RUA ABI ALAA AL MAARI
Jnane Palace Hotel
RUE AHMED CHAOUKI
RUE MED BENJALLOUN
PLACE ALLAL AL FASSI
IBN JARIR
RUE BENZAKOUR
RUE KANDAR
RUE MOULAY SLIMANE
RUE MELLILIA
RUE TANGER
BOULEVARD MOULAY RACHID
RUA AL ADARISSA
AVE HUSSEIN DE JORDAINE
AVE MOHAMED ZERKTOUNI
AVE BOU RKAIZ
& Sefrou

POI
Information
Police Station
Airport
Railway Stn
Bus Station
Hospital

dance and photography exhibitions at various venues throughout the city. Salons and talks are held here in their head office in the Ville Nouvelle. ⓐ 33 rue Loukili ⓣ (035) 62 39 21 or 62 35 40 ⓦ www.institutfrancaisfes.com ◷ 08.30–12.15, 14.30–18.30 Mon–Fri

Instituto Cervantes de Fès

This branch of the worldwide Spanish institution holds exhibitions and film screenings. ⓐ 5 rue Douiat ⓣ (035) 73 20 04 ⓦ http://fez.cervantes.es ◷ 08.30–12.15, 14.30–18.30 Mon–Fri

Orientalist Art Gallery

This cool, white independent exhibition space is the only gallery showcasing contemporary art in Fez. The calibre and variety of the artists displayed make this a worthwhile visit. ⓐ 38 rue Abdelaziz Boutaleb ⓣ (035) 94 45 45 ⓦ www.fes-artgallery.net ◷ 09.30–12.30, 15.30–19.30 Mon–Sat

RETAIL THERAPY

Rafinity This slick, contemporary jewellery boutique sits opposite the Jnane Palace Hotel, and you quickly get a very clear idea about the quality of the bling on offer here when you see the armed guard. Those with money to spend at leisure, away from the prying eyes of the Medina, won't be disappointed by the designs or the gemstones here. Those on a more modest budget can still have plenty of fun looking around and maybe even jotting down a few hints for the Christmas list. ⓐ 12 av. Ahmed Chaouki ⓣ (035) 62 47 48 ◷ 10.00–21.00

QUEEN OF FASSI HEARTS

It's not just Fez that's moving into the modern era – its royalty is becoming fashionable as well. King Mohammed VI succeeded to the throne in 1999 and has proved to be immensely popular. Forward-thinking and passionate about modernising his country, the king has been keen to swell Morocco's coffers by placing particular emphasis on the development of tourism.

But you know what they say: standing squarely beside every great man is a significant other, and, these days, all regal interest tends to centre on Mohammed's better half. Princess Lalla Salma Bennani was born in the Ville Nouvelle in 1978. Although her father was a primary school teacher rather than the usual rich businessman or politician, Bennani got herself well educated and embarked upon a career as a computer engineer. Gifted as she no doubt was at the 'have you tried switching it off and on again?' routine, it seems that Bennani also has the talent and charisma to assume a statesperson-like role. Under Moroccan law kings can take up to four wives, but Mohammed has settled for just one and broken precedent by giving her an official title: Princess Consort to the King of Morocco. Bennani, who was named one of the 'Young Global Leaders of 2008', has boosted the new-found fashionability of Fez in general and of the Ville Nouvelle in particular.

TAKING A BREAK

8 £ ❶ A great spot for breakfast or lunch at any time of the day, this stylish Ville Nouvelle hangout has retro white 70s plastic seating, abundant salads and great pricing. It's popular among the hip set. ⓐ 8 rue Ibn Rushd, Champs Courses ◷ Opening hours vary

Arena Palace £ ❷ This popular café is a prime spot for a breakfast of delicious pastries and coffee overlooking a park. ⓐ 1 av. Allal ben Abdullah ⓣ (035) 94 35 82 ◷ Opening hours vary

La Villa £ ❸ Set within the chic part of the new town, this café, patisserie and boulangerie has an ever-popular sprawling terrace downstairs and does a fantastic breakfast and lunch. Wi-Fi makes it a hit among connected locals. ⓐ Av. Allal ben Abdullah ◷ Opening hours vary

AFTER DARK

RESTAURANTS

Kiotori ££ ❹ This upmarket restaurant opposite the Jnane Palace Hotel is part of the new wave of 21st-century dining options opening in Fez. Beautiful interiors feature traditional Japanese styling and floor-to-ceiling windows overlooking the grounds beyond. There's an array of fresh sushi and Japanese dishes. Takeaway and delivery is available; alcohol is not. ⓐ 12 rue Ahmed Chaouki ⓣ (035) 65 17 00 ◷ 12.00–15.00, 20.00–23.30

Enjoy mint tea and Moroccan cakes in the patisseries of Ville Nouvelle

Zen Garden ££ ❺ A popular spot boasting slick interiors and a lovely garden terrace, Zen Garden mixes a menu of traditional Moroccan dishes with Asiatic bites and its famous pizza in posh surroundings. Cocktails are a further bonus. ⓐ 26 av. Omar Ibnou el Khattab ⓣ (035) 93 29 29 ⓦ www.zengarden.ma ⓛ 12.00–00.00

Le Majestic £££ ❻ One of Fez's most renowned restaurants lies within the Henri Leconte Tennis Academy, serving international *haute cuisine* in a classic setting. With one of the city's best wine lists, the restaurant will transport you from your hotel and drop you home afterwards. ⓐ Henri Leconte Tennis Academy, route de Zwagha ⓣ (035) 72 99 99 ⓦ www.lemajestic.net ⓛ 12.00–15.00, 20.00–23.30

Les Trois Sources £££ ❼ This esteemed restaurant has been popular among gourmets for aeons. With its French menu and three pools, trio of dining rooms and lush gardens, this is luxury. The fish here is particularly good. There's a free taxi service to and from the restaurant. ⓐ Route d'Immouzzer ⓣ (035) 60 65 31 ⓛ 11.00–15.00, 19.00–23.00

BARS & CLUBS

Felix This sprawling disco is where young Moroccans head for a night of drinking and dancing after hours. With plentiful leather seating and strobe lighting, the interiors have seen better days but it nevertheless remains one of the most popular spots for spruced-up locals looking to dance the night away. ⓐ Hotel Tghat, av. des F.A.R. ⓣ (035) 93 06 93 ⓦ www.hotel-tghat.ma ⓛ 23.00–04.00

Le Phoebus The most upmarket of Fez's discothèques, and with prohibitive pricing to match, the Jnane Palace is where the city's rich head for a night on the tiles. It's the closest Fez gets to the European idea of a nightclub, with strobe lighting, alcohol aplenty, a state-of-the-art sound system and seating surrounding the dance floor. DJs spin a selection of club tracks. ⓐ Jnane Palace Hotel, av. Ahmed Chaouki ⓣ (035) 65 22 30 ⓦ www.sogatour.ma ⓛ 22.30–03.00 Tues–Sun

VIP Club With an 80s feel to the red-and-white decoration, plasma screens, live DJ and strobe lighting, this place is a hit with the older crowd, who remember it in its better days. ⓐ Crown Plaza Hotel, av. des F.A.R. ⓣ (035) 93 06 93 ⓛ 23.30–04.00

European dining at Le Majestic

Volubilis This perhaps slightly down-at-heel but nevertheless charming club in the basement of a hotel has lounge seating lining the room and a grown-up, cosmopolitan clientele. Good for cocktails, there's a laid-back feel earlier on, with the tempo picking up after midnight when dance tracks are thrown on and guests take to the floor. Despite the palm tree motif décor and strobe lighting, it feels strangely chic. ⓐ Hotel Volubilis, av. Allal ben Abdullah ⓣ (035) 62 11 26 ◷ 22.00–03.00 Mon–Sat

The alluring blue streets of Chefchaouen

OUT OF TOWN trips

Meknes

Morocco's third imperial city often gets overshadowed by its older, bigger, brasher cousin, Fez. Situated less than an hour away, here you'll find wide roads, a relatively easy-to-navigate Medina, sights and attractions from the reign of Moulay Ismail, *riads* and hassle-free shopping. Meknes's pedestrian zone is peppered with eating and drinking options and after-dark entertainment. The historic city was founded in the 11th century, originally as a military settlement, and designated a World Heritage site in 1996. Just a short journey away are Volubilis (also a World Heritage site) and Moulay Idriss – by turn the oldest and most holy sites in Morocco (see page 112).

GETTING THERE

Meknes is just 50 minutes by train from the railway station in Fez's Ville Nouvelle (see page 50). A first class ticket costs around 26dh; second class costs 18dh. There are 11 trains per day. Meknes has three railway stations; for the old town, alight at Meknes Al Amir. Another option is to take a *grand* taxi from Fez's Gare Routière outside the Medina (see page 51). The journey time is the same and it costs around 25dh for a seat. When in Meknes, the *grand* taxi station is just outside the gates to the south of the old town, and from here you can travel back to Fez or take a ride across the hill to Volubilis and Moulay Idriss, which lie a pleasant 4 km (2 ½ mile) walk apart from each another. If you are driving, take the N6 motorway heading southwest to reach Meknes. Additionally, there are tour operators in Fez who will

Stroll under the ancient arches of the Granaries

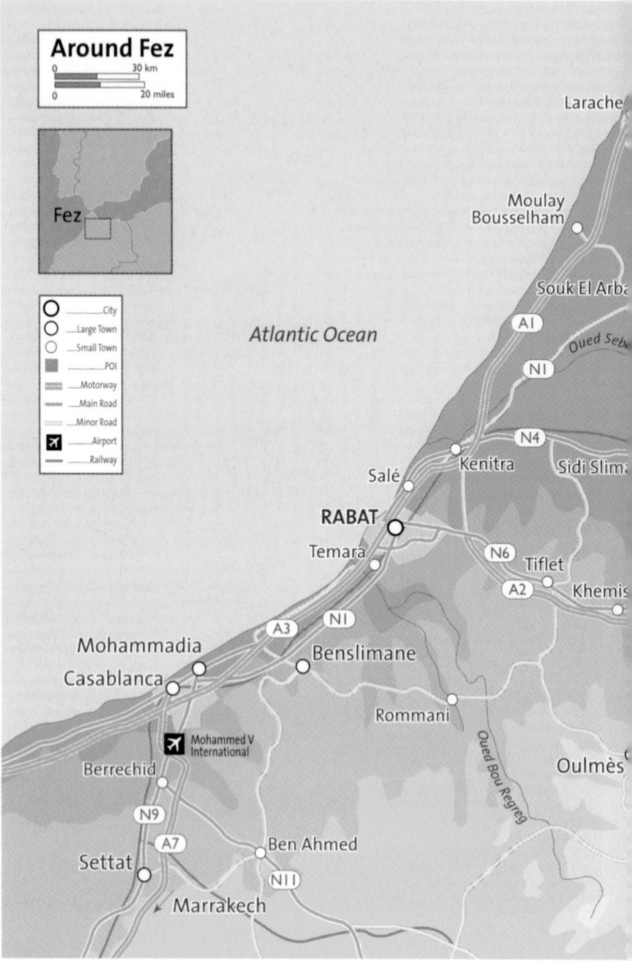

Around Fez

0 30 km
0 20 miles

Fez

City
Large Town
Small Town
POI
Motorway
Main Road
Minor Road
Airport
Railway

Atlantic Ocean

Larache
Moulay Bousselham
Souk El Arb
A1
Oued Seb
N1
N4
Kenitra
Sidi Slim
Salé
RABAT
Temara
N6
Tiflet
A2
Khemis
N1
A3
Mohammadia
Benslimane
Casablanca
Rommani
Mohammed V International
Oued Bou Regreg
Oulmès
Berrechid
N9
A7
Ben Ahmed
Settat
N11
Marrakech

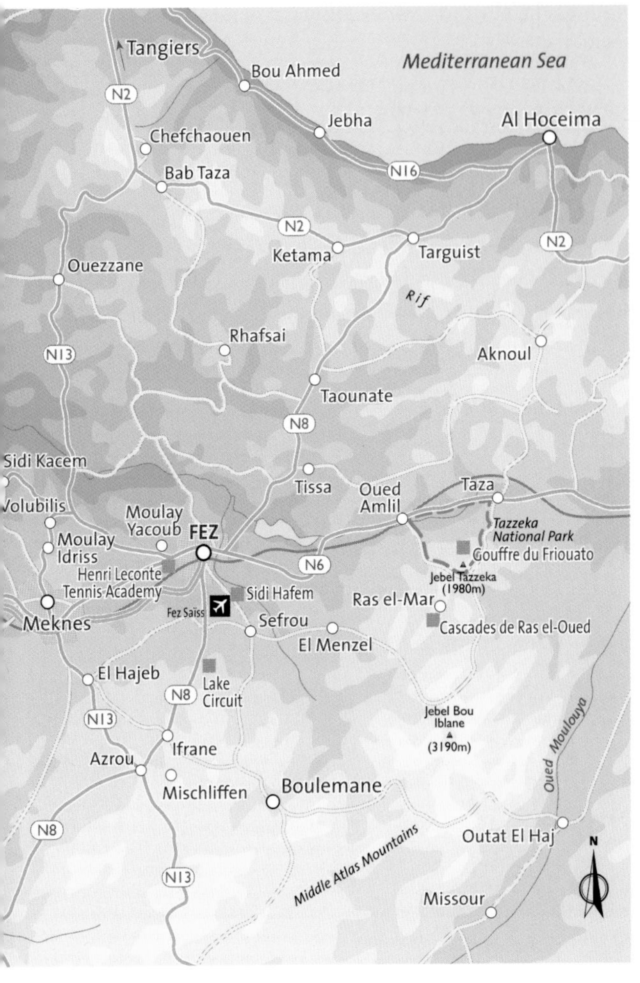
Tangiers
Bou Ahmed
Mediterranean Sea
N2
Jebha
Al Hoceima
Chefchaouen
Bab Taza
N16
N2
Ketama
Targuist
N2
Ouezzane
Rif
Rhafsai
Aknoul
N13
Taounate
N8
Sidi Kacem
Tissa
Oued Amlil
Taza
Volubilis
Moulay Yacoub
FEZ
Tazzeka National Park
Moulay Idriss
Gouffre du Friouato
N6
Henri Leconte Tennis Academy
Jebel Tazzeka (1980m)
Sidi Hafem
Ras el-Mar
Fez Saïss
Meknes
Sefrou
Cascades de Ras el-Oued
El Menzel
El Hajeb
Lake Circuit
N8
Jebel Bou Iblane (3190m)
N13
Ifrane
Oued Moulouya
Azrou
Mischliffen
Boulemane
N8
Outat El Haj
Middle Atlas Mountains
N
N13
Missour

arrange the transport and guide you around all three attractions in one day.

SIGHTS & ATTRACTIONS

Bab el-Mansour

The greatest gates in Africa lie in Meknes – three Palladian arches whose mosaics glimmer in the sunlight and form a great, sweeping portal between the Medina and the Ville Nouvelle. Bab el-Mansour makes for a magisterial frame around Place el-Hedim. Inside there are sometimes art exhibitions.

The huge gate of Bab el-Mansour

Bou Inania Medersa

This now-defunct *medersa* next to the Grand Mosque gives you a glimpse of what scholastic life was like many centuries ago. Pigeonhole bedrooms line the upper floor, entered via keyhole silhouette doorways. Their views onto the *medersa* below are glorious. 09.00–12.00, 15.00–19.00. Admission charge

Calèche Ride

One of the most genteel ways to see Meknes is to hire a horse and cart and trot around the city in one of these gaily decorated vehicles. The two-hour journey sets off from the Granaries or the entrance to Place El Hedim, near Bab Mansour, and will typically set you back 150dh.

Heri es-Souani

These awesome granaries and stables, built by the legendary Moulay Ismail, are a feat of human endeavour. Must-see features are sophisticated underground irrigation systems and arching domed ceilings that were designed to create a perpetually cool climate for the giant stores. There is space enough to stable 12,000 horses in the lovely (but dilapidated) arched gardens beyond. 09.00–18.00. Admission charge

Koubbat el-Khiyatin (Koubbat as-Sufara)

Deep underground, around the corner from Place el-Hedim, lie cavernous cellars beneath a large reception room which used to welcome foreign ambassadors. According to legend, the cellars were once used as a prison for Christians. When you visit you feel horror at the thought of the captives imprisoned

VOLUBILIS & MOULAY IDRISS

A short drive from Meknes lies the holiest town in Morocco, Moulay Idriss. It was created by its namesake, the founder of Islam in Morocco, as he was waiting for Fez to be built. His tomb remains here inside a shrine. So sacred that non-Muslims were not even allowed to enter before 1920, it's a fascinating pilgrimage site as well as being the site of Morocco's premier religious festival, the Moussem Moulay Idriss. With its tiny *medina* and ancient ways, the town feels like it hasn't changed in a thousand years. It probably hasn't.

Just four miles away, on top of a hill, lies Volubilis. The capital of a Berber kingdom before being claimed by Roman invaders, it is the oldest Roman settlement in North Africa. A feast of intricacy, the vast remains of this city are astonishing in their scope and detail. It's a UNESCO World Heritage site, and well worth a visit.

underground. A less frightening and probably truer alternative is that these cellars were actually food stores. Fact or fiction, it makes for an unforgettable visit. ◷ 09.00–18.00. Admission charge

Moulay Ismail Zawiya

One of the few mausoleums that non-Muslims can enter. The resting place of Meknes's former tyrant Sultan Moulay Ismail of Morocco is daubed in soothing aqua mosaics and inlaid with cool marble. While tourists still can't enter the shrine room itself, it's clearly visible, with the bodies of the sultan and his wife and son laid to rest in the centre of the room. ⓐ South of pl. Lalla Aouda

CULTURE

Musée Dar Jamaï

This beautiful *riad* museum was once the palace of Moulay Ismail. Today it houses fascinating artefacts from Meknes's past in the chambers surrounding the exquisite walled gardens. ⓐ Pl. el-Hedim (north side) ⓣ (035) 53 31 46 ⓛ 09.30–19.00 (closed Fri afternoons)

RETAIL THERAPY

Antique Shop This fascinating antique shop specialises in historical and religious items originating from Morocco's Jewry, from old *torahs* to parchment scrolls and jewellery to musical instruments. ⓐ 3 Bis Tiberbarine ⓣ (035) 53 31 46 ⓛ 09.30–21.00 (closed Fri afternoons)

Jewellery Kissariat This square has some of the finest jewellery, not to mention prices, in the array of booth-like shops in Morocco. Pick up contemporary and classic designs from modest to opulent in this glittering *souk*. Be prepared to haggle. It's close to the Grand Mosque near the entrance from Place el-Hedim.

Olive Shop Truly a sight to behold. Set within the lively food *souk*, the stall at the end occupies an entire row, selling all manner of

olives in picturesque pyramids and spicy combinations. It's one of the most popular stops on the Meknes trail. ⓐ Pl. el-Hedim ◷ 09.00–22.00

Sewing quarter A feast of colour awaits you in the embroiderers' *souk*. It's situated close to the entrance of the Medina from Place el-Hedim.

TAKING A BREAK

Collier de la Colombe £ This charming courtyard café restaurant is tucked behind Bab Mansour. It has terraces overlooking the river and good traditional Moroccan food. It is enduringly popular, and rightly so. ⓐ 67 rue Driba ⓣ (035) 55 50 41 ◷ Opening hours vary

Place el-Hedim £ The cafés lining the vast square presided over by Bab Mansour and bordering the Medina are popular spots for coffee, orange juice and people-watching.

Sweet Sultana £ As the name might suggest, this is an unashamed tourist stop, attached to a guesthouse behind the Musée Dar Jamaï. Nevertheless, it serves up solid Moroccan food in charmingly garish Moorish surrounds. During the evening there are belly-dancers providing entertainment, and there is a nice terrace upstairs for mint tea throughout the day. ⓐ 4 Derb Sekkaya, Tiberbarine ⓣ (035) 53 57 20 ⓦ www.dar-sultana.com ◷ Opening hours vary

Plenty of produce at the food souk *in Meknes*

AFTER DARK

Le Relais de Paris £ Mountain views, good service and a no-nonsense set menu for just 110dh – one of the best formulas in Meknes. A lovely garden and lounge are just a couple of this veteran restaurant's other charms. ⓐ 46 rue Okba bin Nafa ⓣ (035) 51 54 88 ⓛ 11.00–23.00

Place el-Hedim £ This square is a must if you're staying late in Meknes. You'll find snake charmers, storytellers, monkeys, transvestite dancers and all manner of entertainers in the heaving square, which bustles with life and colour after dark and has an array of restaurants and food stands from which to survey the action.

La Case ££ Iberian – yes, Iberian – hues and rustic simplicity provide the backdrop to this acclaimed restaurant. The bouquets are the region's finest, and the French-Italian menu features well-cooked meat and fish alongside a fine selection of crepes. It's situated a short stroll from the train station. ⓐ 8 blvd Moulay Youssef ⓣ (035) 52 40 19 ⓛ 12.00–15.00, 19.00–23.00 Mon–Sat

Riad D'Or ££ Fantastic eating and drinking possibilities sprawl across the various stylish salons and terraces of this designer *riad*, where the conviviality and service are second to none. ⓐ 17 rue Ain el-Anboub, Quartier Hammam ⓣ (041) 07 86 25 ⓦ www.riaddor.com ⓛ Opening hours vary

ACCOMMODATION

Riad Felloussia £ One of the best stays in Meknes, Felloussia is set within a charmingly restored *riad*. Some rooms feature *hammam* bathrooms or mezzanine beds. The views over the Medina and its surrounding areas are peerless. ⓐ Derb Hammam el-Jdid, Bab Aissi ⓣ (035) 53 08 40 ⓦ http://riadmeknes.blogspot.com

Ryad Bahia £ This gem was the first *riad* hotel to open in Meknes, and the English-speaking owners are only too happy to help. Four bedrooms accommodate up to eight people, ensuring a convivial air. Henna and *hammams* are also on the menu. ⓐ Tiberbarine ⓣ (035) 55 45 41 ⓦ www.ryad-bahia.com

Palais Didi ££ A reliable option, and one of Meknes's *grand dames*, Didi is housed in a 17th-century palace. With a range of individually designed rooms and suites, it offers fantastic views from the terrace over the Medina and royal golf course. ⓐ 7 Dar el-Kebira ⓣ (055) 55 85 90 ⓦ www.palaisdidi.com

Riad D'Or ££ This Italian-owned *riad* could be a museum, and the trendy terrace and fashionable touches add a hint of style. ⓐ 17 rue Ain el-Anboub, Quartier Hammam ⓣ (041) 07 86 25 ⓦ www.riaddor.com

Head for the Heights

If the heat's getting too much and the *medinas* too narrow, head for the heights of the Middle Atlas with their legendary mountain air and beautiful surroundings. As well as being rejuvenated and invigorated by the great outdoors, you'll meet Berbers and Barbary apes and can even swim in lakes and ski on mountains. Chefchaouen, one of the main towns in the Rif Mountains, is also one of the most enchanting in Morocco.

GETTING THERE

All the destinations in this chapter can be reached easily by car: the closest, Moulay Yacoub, is half an hour away while the furthest, Chefchaouen, is a four-hour drive away. Do be warned that roads can be rough and winding, and in some places precipitous.

To reach Chefchaouen, take the R50 and R48 routes north until you reach the N13 motorway. Follow this northbound to the end. For Tazzeka, a two-and-a-half hour drive away, take the N6 route east until you come to Taza, then head south on the R507. Ifrane and Azrou lie around a 15-minute drive away from each other. Take the N13 south up the mountain from Fez and you will reach both destinations in just over one hour. Sefrou is located around a half hour drive from Fez, heading south along the R503. Moulay Yacoub is a 20-minute drive north along the R503. If you want to take a cab, *grands* taxis for the more far-flung destinations leave from the CTM hub in the Ville Nouvelle, while transport to Sefrou and Moulay Yacoub can be caught from outside the Gare Routière near the Medina.

Visit colourful Chefchaouen in the Rif Mountains

AZROU

The Berber town of Azrou, 17 km (10 ½ miles) from Ifrane, is a popular spot for a snoop around the Tuesday market. There is an impressive array of carpets made by villagers, whose prices are much lower than those found in Fez. Azrou is also the gate to the cedar forests in the Middle Atlas. These are a joy to explore, not least because of the

Azrou stretches across the mountain landscape

DOORWAY TO THE MIDDLE ATLAS

The areas surrounding Sefrou, Ifrane and Tazzeka are considered the doorway to the Middle Atlas. The range accounts for nearly a fifth of Morocco's mountains and is interspersed with cedar forests and volcanic plateaus. The stronghold of the Berber tribes, it encompasses gorges, ski-slopes, lakes and sulphurous waters. This remarkable terrain is thought to have been created by slow-moving tectonic plates.

Barbary apes, which can usually be spotted on a guided hike. Plentiful small villages abound and from these you can buy trinkets or sample some of the legendary local fare with a delicious Berber-cooked meal.

SIGHTS & ATTRACTIONS

Cedar Forests

Bordering Azrou, these are the home to Morocco's legendary Barbary apes (which are, in fact, macaque monkeys). The forests are a joy to wander, and your chances of spotting a passing posse are high. Some are relatively tame and will even let you feed them by hand.

Tuesday Market

The Tuesday central market here is a popular out-of-town destination. Visitors can witness a snippet of real Berber lifestyle and snap up some carpets and handicrafts at a steal.

CHEFCHAOUEN

The furthest away from Fez, but definitely worth the trek, this laid-back mountain town is set around 5,000 metres (16,404 ft) above sea level in the Rif Mountains. It ranks among the top tourist destinations in Morocco. Its striking Medina is peppered with red roofs and blue buildings, a convergence of its Moroccan and Andalusian past. For centuries, it was a refuge for Jews and Muslims fleeing Spain, and was actually occupied by the Spanish in 1920; before that time, Europeans entered at their own risk. Today the Muslim inhabitants still speak Spanish.

Explore the shops in the winding streets of Chefchaouen

SIGHTS & ATTRACTIONS

Medina

Chefchaouen's *medina*, distinctively blue and red, is almost impossibly pretty. Tiny labyrinthine streets and friendly Inhabitants make for an intimate, welcoming place.

TAKING A BREAK

La Lampe Magique £ Enchanting restaurant overlooking the Plaza Uta el-Hammam serving regional dishes in captivating surroundings. ⓐ Rue Targui ⓛ Opening hours vary

Restaurant Al-Azhar £ Handily located café for considering market buys that serves a range of fish dishes, unusual for this part of town. ⓐ Av. Moulay Idriss ⓛ Opening hours vary

ACCOMMODATION

Hotel Madrid £ A cosy, traditional 2-star hotel in the town centre. ⓐ Avenue Hassan II ⓣ (039) 98 74 96

Hotel Atlas Chaouen ££ A fine 3-star hotel with 70 rooms, a restaurant, bar and nightclub and a health spa. ⓐ Rue Sidi Abdelhamid ⓣ (039) 98 60 02 ⓦ www.hotelsatlas.com

IFRANE

Head out to Ifrane, set high in the mountains, and the clean, restorative air instantly hits you. Moroccans are enchanted by this place and its cool temperatures, abundant conifers and Swiss architecture, and it's a popular weekend getaway for

Fassis and Casablancans alike. Europeans may find this relic of the French occupancy a touch on the twee side, but it's a cool spot for a bite on the way to the two natural attractions bordering it – the Mischliffen ski slope and the lakes. These make it a good activity destination to visit during the summer and winter months.

SIGHTS & ATTRACTIONS

Mischliffen

This ski resort lies a few kilometres south of Ifrane and is the most famous in Morocco. In recent years the snow has become noticeably thinner; however, during the winter months there's usually some snow on the piste. Situated 2,100 m (6,890 ft) above sea-level, the air is sublime.

The Lake Circuit

A great place to take a dip or to savour the mountain air via a lakeside walk, this sequence of five pretty lakes 12 km (7 ½ miles) away from Ifrane is home to herons, egrets and coots. You'll find the best variety of wildlife by Lac Dayet Aoua (considered to be among the most beautiful waterways in the whole of Morocco) and in the cedar forests around it, where you might come across birds of prey, a troupe of Barbary apes or even a jackal if you're lucky.

TAKING A BREAK

Cookie Craque **£–££** A popular American-owned café-cum-restaurant that sits on the town's square. It serves a range of dishes including pizza, but crêpes and ice creams are

its number-one lure. Ⓐ Av. des Tilleuls Ⓣ (035) 56 71 71
Ⓛ 07.00–22.00 Mon–Fri, 07.00–23.30 Sat & Sun

Chalet du Lac ££ This restaurant on Lac Dayet Aoua serves fantastic food in hearty four-course sittings. Renowned as the area's best stop for lunch or dinner, there's an intriguing menu and the bonus of basic rooms upstairs in the chalet, should you need to sleep off your meal. Days and hours of opening vary, so be sure to phone ahead. Ⓐ North side of Lac Dayet Aoua, Immouzzer du Kandar Ⓣ (035) 66 32 77

JEBEL TAZZEKA & AROUND

A two-and-a-half-hour drive away from Fez, the areas surrounding Morocco's newest national park contain waterfalls, gorges and, perhaps most significantly, the deepest cave in North Africa. The closest town is Taza.

SIGHTS & ATTRACTIONS

Cascades de Ras el Oued

These waterfalls are at their most impressive in early spring, as the snow caps from the Middle Atlas melt and spring showers add to the flow.

Gouffre du Friouato

Arguably the area's biggest draw, this cave near Taza is said to be the deepest in North Africa, at over 20 m (65 ½ ft) wide and 100 m (328 ft) deep. There are over 700 steps to the bottom, and once at ground zero you must squeeze through a hole to

descend further and begin investigating the other-wordly chambers below. The guardian of the caves, Mostapha Lachhab, will gladly show you around. You are strongly urged to take a guide when exploring beyond the mouth of the cave. ⓐ Tazzeka National Park

Tazzeka National Park
A must for hikers, this expansive national park is Morocco's newest, with a range of attractions and wonderful oak forests.

MOULAY YACOUB

Of the two spa towns bordering Fez on the route to the Middle Atlas, Moulay Yacoub is the better known. A pretty car or *grand* taxi ride past fields and villages leads to an attraction beloved by families and health enthusiasts alike. The waters here are said to be curative, produced as they are by volcanic thermal springs running up through the mountains and thus rich in sulphur, magnesium, calcium and sodium. There are various public pools in addition to the Jnane Palace-run Moulay Yacoub Wellness (see below). These offer a big difference in price – 15dh as opposed to 90dh for the private pools.

SIGHTS & ATTRACTIONS

Moulay Yacoub Wellness
This sprawling centre is not quite as glossy as the brochures make it out to be, but the feeling of wellness induced by a dip in the naturally warm waters of the spherical pool and its overhead massage jets leaves you feeling remarkably buff.

Hebrew inscriptions on the walls of the Sefrou Synagogue

Don't be scared by the unisex changing rooms and contraptions designed to target and flood various parts of the body with the healing waters of Moulay Yacoub. Be warned – the road here is out of the way at the base of a huge hill, so don't attempt it unless you have your own vehicle: you might have problems getting back! ⓐ Moulay Yacoub ⓣ (055) 69 40 35 ⓦ www.sogatour.ma ⓛ 09.00–19.00

SEFROU

The Berber village of Sefrou predates Fez and makes for a pretty detour. Its tiny *medina* is far easier to navigate, the feel is authentic and untouched and the river flowing through it creates an open feel. The town was originally inhabited by Berbers of Jewish descent. Indeed, the *medina* once held one of Morocco's largest Jewish communities (around 8,000 people), and its *mellah* is a must-see on your visit. Today, Sefrou is famous for producing the finest cherries in Morocco, and its annual Cherry Harvest Festival is famous throughout the land.

RETAIL THERAPY

Nany Cerise If you've been dithering over whether to purchase a *jellaba* in Fez but unsure as to its sway back home, be sure to check out the caftan boutique Nany Cerise, which offers an array of fitted designs featuring the embroidery for which Sefrou is renowned. ⓣ (061) 52 27 71 or 73 52 80 ⓛ Opening hours vary

Don't worry, it's easy to understand the signs

PRACTICAL
information

Directory

GETTING THERE

By air

Fez is served by the national carrier **Royal Air Maroc** (www.royalairmaroc.com), with flights departing from Canada (Montreal), the UK (London Gatwick) and the US (New York). All flights stop at Casablanca en route to Fez. The average total journey time from Gatwick to Fez Saïss is seven hours. Alternative airports include Casablanca, around four hours away by train, Marrakech, which is just over seven hours away by train, and Tangiers.

Another option is low-cost carriers such as **Jet4You** (www.jet4you.com), which flies direct from Paris Orly. **Ryanair** (www.ryanair.com) flies from Barcelona, Brussels, Frankfurt, Marseilles and Milan, while **Atlas Blue** (www.atlas-blue.com), operates out of Lyon and Marseilles.

Many people are aware that air travel emits CO_2, which contributes to climate change. You may be interested in the possibility of lessening the environmental impact of your flight through **Climate Care** (www.climatecare.org), which offsets your CO_2 by funding environmental projects around the world.

By rail

The Moroccan rail network is safe and reliable. Its website (www.oncf.ma) has full details of all journeys, routes and fares. The best way of travelling to Fez by rail from Europe is to catch a direct train from Tangiers after taking the ferry from Gibraltar (see opposite). There are four trains a day and the

Riad Dar-echchouan

journey takes about five hours. A first-class seat costs 145dh, a second-class pew 97dh.

By road

The best way of driving to Fez from outside Morocco is to take the N2 motorway south from Tangiers after alighting from the ferry and then following the N13, which leads you to Fez.

By ferry

Several ferry companies make the crossing from Spain to Morocco. These include **Euroferrys** (www.euroferrys.com), which crosses from Algeciras (a four-hour journey). The fastest route when travelling by sea is to take the **Ferries Rapido del Sur** service

Trains run to Fez from cities such as Marrakech and Tangiers

(www.frs.es), which takes 35 minutes from Tarifa, 70 minutes from Algeciras and 80 minutes from Gibraltar to Tangiers.

ENTRY FORMALITIES

All visitors to Morocco should ensure that their passport is valid for at least six months after their date of arrival. For citizens of Australia, Canada, the European Union (except foreign nationals living in the Republic of Ireland), New Zealand, the UK and the USA there are no visa requirements for visits of up to three months. South Africans and foreign nationals residing in the Republic of Ireland should contact their consulates or embassies (see page 139) for further information surrounding entry requirements.

One bottle of spirits and one bottle of wine is the maximum amount of alcohol that can be brought into the country by an adult; 200 cigarettes, 250 grams of tobacco or 50 cigars is the tobacco limit. Non-commercial personal possessions (such as cameras) can be brought into Morocco duty free.

MONEY

Morocco's currency is the dirham, often represented as 'dh'. Notes come in denominations of 20, 50, 100 and 200 dirham, while coins are in 5, 10 and 20 centimes, and 0.5, 1.5 and 10 dirham. One dirham equals 100 centimes.

Moroccan currency must not be taken out of the country. Currency can be resold at banks, bureaux de change and in hotels alongside presentation of the initial transaction receipt.

The euro is frequently accepted in hotels and restaurants, and sometimes favourable when shopping in *souks*. Prices are often given in euros alongside dirhams. Many banks include exchange bureaux, while ATMs are common in towns. However they don't always work and not all accept foreign cards.

Credit cards are accepted at the more expensive hotels, as well as the most upmarket restaurants and shops.

HEALTH, SAFETY & CRIME

No vaccinations are needed for Morocco. It's wise only to drink bottled water and wash fruit and vegetables. Use plenty of sun protection in the summer.

The teachings of Islam do much to guarantee that violent crimes are rare. However, women may occasionally encounter individuals who appear intimidating. If someone tries to coerce you into giving them money or taking them on as a 'guide', simply ignore them or firmly refuse. If there are no tourist police around (see page 139) and you're frightened, go into a shop, café or other place of business and make it clear that you are being hassled. Help will be at hand.

Wandering around any of Fez's major or busy thoroughfares tends to be safe during the day, though it's wise to avoid venturing into isolated byways and areas, particularly as a woman. It's easy to get lost, particularly at night, so be sure to stick to the main arteries. At night, women may not feel comfortable walking alone in the streets and in the Medina. Wherever possible they should take a taxi directly to their destination. When asking for directions at night it is safer to give the name of the area you are trying to reach than a specific hotel or address.

Fez's Medina is a destination of religious importance. Thus it is respectful, and more comfortable, to dress modestly. Don't wear too much jewellery or display valuables, and don't carry more money than is necessary for a day out.

OPENING HOURS

Typical opening hours for private offices are 08.00–12.00 and 14.00–18.00 from Monday to Friday, while banks are usually open between 08.15 and 15.45 on weekdays.

Shops in the Ville Nouvelle tend to stick to a fairly set regime of 09.30–12.30 and 14.30–20.30 Monday to Thursday, with days and hours varying between Friday and Sunday. In the Medina shops are generally open 09.00–19.00, however some will have longer hours. *Souks* tend to stay open until around 22.00. Most shops within the Medina are closed for all or part of the day on Fridays. Museum times also vary, but in general are open 09.00–18.00 or 19.00 from Saturday to Thursday.

TOILETS

There are very few public toilets in Fez, so if you're *in extremis* it's best to stop at a café, restaurant or hotel and request the use of their facilities.

CHILDREN

While children occupy a special place in the hearts of Fassis and of Moroccans generally, travelling with the very young in the Medina will most likely not be easy. Here, hazards such as working animals, people carrying heavy loads and substantial human traffic make navigating tiny, uneven, bumpy streets with young children difficult. Using pushchairs is nearly impossible. However, the clearer, wider roads towards the east of the Medina in Batha, Bou Jeloud, Ziat and the top of Talaa Kebira are the safest and easiest to traverse, while all the areas outside the Medina except Al-Andalous should be comfortable to navigate.

Open spaces such as Jnane Sbil (see page 87), the Merenid Tombs (see page 88), Borj Nord and Borj Sud (see page 90) make for child-friendly destinations, while the Fondouk Americain (see page 87) and Art Naji pottery workshops (see page 88) are sure to delight the young.

COMMUNICATIONS

Internet

There are many internet cafés in the Medina and Ville Nouvelle. Two reliable options are:

Bathanet Opposite the police station in the Batha area of the Medina, this is a popular internet café that's open until late.

TELEPHONING MOROCCO

When calling Morocco from abroad, dial the local international code (typically 00) followed by 212. Then drop the first zero from the local code before dialling the number you require. For Fez, you would dial 00 212 35 followed by the local telephone number.

TELEPHONING ABROAD

Dialling abroad from Morocco follows the same rule as in most other countries: dial the international code 00, followed by the code of the country you wish to reach. For Australia it's 61, for Canada and the USA 1, for the Republic of Ireland 353, for New Zealand 64, South Africa 27 and for the UK 44. The number for international operator services is 120, while for national enquiries dial 160.

There's the option to use an English-layout keyboard. ⓐ 14 rue de la Poste ⓑ 09.00–00.00

Cybernet This chic little cybercafé is the best of its type in the Ville Nouvelle. ⓐ Blvd Mohammed V ⓑ 09.00–00.00

Post

The Central Post Office is located on the junction of Avenue Mohammed V and Boulevard Hassan II in the Ville Nouvelle. There are others on Batha Square in the Medina and Alaouite Square in el-Jdid. Staff are usually helpful and some speak English.

Stamps can be bought in most kiosks and news-stands around town. Letters and cards can be posted in the bright yellow post boxes (both freestanding and attached to buildings). To be sure that your post will arrive overseas, deposit it in one of the boxes directly within the post offices.

ELECTRICITY

Electricity in Fez largely works on 110 volts, although some plugs operate in line with Western Europe, with 220 volts (AC) and 50 hertz. Standard round-ended two-pin adapters used on the Continent are needed for UK and US equipment.

TRAVELLERS WITH DISABILITIES

Travellers with severe disabilities may find the Medina difficult to navigate. Streets are labyrinthine and uneven and there are frequently people and animals carrying heavy loads that wait for no-one. Most buildings are reached via steps, and only a couple of the hotels in the Medina can accommodate disabled visitors. The facilities in the Ville Nouvelle are more amenable, with smoother thoroughfares, ramp systems and lifts operating in many of the hotels.

TOURIST INFORMATION

The main **Fez Tourist Board** (t (035) 62 34 60 ⏲ 08.30–12.00, 14.30–18.30) can be found on Place d'Istiqlal at the junction of Avenue Moulay Youssef and Place de la Resistance. The **Tourist Information Office** (t (035) 62 47 69) is situated on Place Mohammed V. There is no tourist office in the Medina. The city's official online guide (w www.visitfes.org) has comprehensive information, although at the time of writing it was only available in French. Morocco's official tourism site is w www.visitmorocco.org.

BACKGROUND READING

Dreams of Trespass: Tales of a Harem Girlhood by Fatima Mernissi. The author's childhood memories of life as a 20th-century Fassi female.
Fez: From Bab to Bab by Hammad Berrada. A must-read guide of walking tours within the Medina.
House in Fez by Suzanna Clarke. True-life account of a modern Antipodean couple who moved to Fez and restored an old *riad*.
Leo the African by Amin Maalouf. The gripping tale of how the famous 16th-century writer and geographer Leo Africanus fled the Spanish inquisition and settled in Fez.
The Spider's House by Paul Bowles. Probably the most acclaimed literary work set in Fez. Taking place in the final days of the French occupation, it contains a vivid depiction of the Medina.

Emergencies

The following are emergency free-call numbers:
Ambulance 15
Fire 15
Police 19

MEDICAL SERVICES

There are two main hospitals in Fez. The **Omar Drissi Hospital** ((035) 63 45 51) in Place de l'Istiqlal is situated in the Medina, while the **Al-Ghassani Hospital University Hassan II** (Dar al-Mahrez (035) 62 27 76) is situated in the Ville Nouvelle. There are chemists all over the Medina and in the Ville Nouvelle, and an **all-night chemist** ((035) 62 33 80) on Avenue Abdelkrim El-Khattabi. You'll see signs for dentists throughout the city.

EMERGENCY PHRASES

Help!	**Fire!**	**Stop!**
Au secours!	Au feu!	Stop!
Ossercoor!	*Oh fur!*	*Stop!*

Call an ambulance/a doctor/the police/the fire service!
Appelez une ambulance/un médecin/la police/ les pompiers!
Ahperleh ewn ahngbewlahngss/ang medesang/lah poleess/ leh pompeeyeh!

POLICE

The main police station in the Medina is situated in rue de la Poste in the Batha area of Fez, and you should make your way here to report a crime.

You will come across the specialist tourist police, whose role it is to watch out for unauthorised guides and other potential tourist hazards. The tourist police are more helpful for day-to-day problems or enquiries than regular police, whom you should call upon if you are the victim of a serious crime. Tourist police dress in blue but are not frequently seen on the streets.

EMBASSIES & CONSULATES

The nearest embassies to Fez are all located in Rabat, with the exception of the Republic of Ireland, whose consulate is in Casablanca, and New Zealand, whose nearest embassy is in Spain. Some major embassies are:

Britain ⓐ 28 av. S.A.R. Sidi Mohammed Souissi, Rabat ⓣ (037) 63 33 33 ⓦ www.britishembassy.gov.uk

Canada & Australia ⓐ 13 bis rue Jaafar As-Sadik, Rabat ⓣ (037) 68 74 00

New Zealand ⓐ Calle del Pinar 7, 28006 Madrid, Spain ⓣ +34 915 230 226 ⓦ www.nzembassy.com

Republic of Ireland ⓐ Copragi Building, blvd Moulay Ismail, route de Rabat, Casablanca ⓣ (022) 66 03 06

South Africa ⓐ 34 rue des Saadiens, Rabat ⓣ (037) 70 67 60 ⓦ www.dfa.gov.za

USA ⓐ 2 av. de Marrakesh, Rabat ⓣ (037) 76 22 65 ⓦ www.usembassy.ma

ACKNOWLEDGEMENTS

Editorial/project management: Lisa Plumridge
Copy editors: Monica Guy and Paul Hines
Layout/DTP: Alison Rayner
Specialist fact checker: Paula Hardy

The publishers would like to thank the following individuals and organisations for supplying their copyright photographs for this book: Anthea, page 89; Lydia Beyoud (http://lallalydia.blogspot.com), page 93; Steve & Jemma Copley, pages 1, 7, 9, 25, 37, 42–3, 45, 47, 57, 73, 74 & 79; Rosanna Downes, page 15; Fotolia (77th Image, page 120; Mohamed El Hajjami, pages 40–1; Alexander Gordeev, page 26; Amin Kane, page 101; Raphael Levy, page 12; Tatiana Pavlova, page 95; Tilo, page 29); Gabirulo, pages 50–1 & 61; Arvind Grover, page 33; C Hugues, pages 105 & 122, Bartlomiej Kwieciszewski/BigStockPhoto.com, page 49; Andrew Larsen, page 17; Brett Lees-Smith, page 59; Olivier Londe, page 90; Le Majestic, page 103; Oliver Mallich, pages 19, 21, 67, 69 & 131; Chris Martin, pages 107, 110 & 129; Paolo, pages 115 & 119; Rosino, pages 23, 65 & 83; Omer Simkha, page 127.